BLACK AND BROWN

Race, Ethnicity, and School Preparation

William A. Sampson

ScarecrowEducation
Lanham, Maryland • Toronto • Oxford
2004

A SCARECROWEDUCATION BOOK

Published in the United States of America
by Scarecrow Press, Inc.
An imprint of The Rowman & Littlefield Publishing Group, Inc.
4501 Forbes Boulevard, Suite 200, Lanham, Maryland 20706
www.scarecrowpress.com

PO Box 317
Oxford
OX2 9RU, UK

British Library Cataloguing in Publication Information Available

Library of Congress Cataloging-in-Publication Data
Sampson, William A., 1946–
    Black and brown : race, ethnicity, and school preparation /
William A. Sampson
        p. cm.
    Includes bibliograhical references and index
    ISBN 1-57886-188-8 (pbk. : alk. paper)
    1. Children of minorities—Education—Illinios—Evanston—Case studies.
    2. Poor children—Education—Illinios—Evanston—Case studies. 3.
    Education—Parent participation—Illinios—Evanston—Case studies. 4.
    Home and school—Illinios—Evanston—Case studies. 5. Academic
    achievement—Illinios—Evanston—Case studies. I. Title
LC3733.E93S36 2005
371.829'00973—dc22

                                                    2004014721

⊗™ The paper used in this publication meets the minimum requirements of
American National Standard for Information Sciences—Permanence of Paper
for Printed Library Materials, ANSI/NISO Z39.48-1992.
Manufactured in the United States of America.

To my beloved uncle, Thomas Marion Armour; my mentor, greatest supporter, and guide, Thomas A. Reynolds Jr.; and all of the poor Latino and poor black parents who struggle each day to properly prepare their children for the educational experience and the world.

CONTENTS

PREFACE

It is referred to as "the gap": the difference in the academic perform-ance of urban black and Latino students and their white counterparts. As Valdes (1998) tells us, "The fact is that the rates of educational at-tainment for Hispanics are very low." According to Irvine (1991), "Poor black students usually score lower on standardized measures of achieve-ment." The gap in the performance on the 2003 National Association of Education Progress Reading Exam for fourth graders between black and white students ranges from fifteen points in the state of Washington to sixty-three points in Washington, D.C. (NAEP 2003). In fact, we in America have come to believe that poor urban Latino and black stu-dents routinely do poorly in the classroom, and we devote a great deal of time and money to change this.

In reality, many poor urban black and Latino students do quite well in the classroom, perhaps not as well as some of their white counter-parts, but they are not all poor performers. We must ask ourselves why some can do well while others in the same income bracket, the same schools, and living in the same neighborhoods do poorly. We know that a difference in intelligence is not the answer; if they attend the same or similar schools, then a difference in schools is not the answer. If they are all lower income, a difference in income is not the answer. We need an answer because if we can understand why some poor Latino and black students do well in school while others do not, then we can perhaps use that information to help others do well too.

Increasingly, the research on the academic performance of poor black and poor Latino students points to the role played by the families of these students in school preparation as a key factor—indeed, perhaps *the* key factor. While the nation looks for ways to make school more effective for these students, as well we should, we also need to pay a great deal more attention to finding ways to make the parents of these children more effective. The reality is that few of the efforts to improve schools have borne fruit on a consistent, widespread basis; when they have, it is often a case of self-selection. That is, the most effective parents tend to find the most effective schools for their children, making it appear that the schools or the techniques are better than they actually are.

Staff stability, a coherent curriculum, a well-trained staff, and sound leadership are all important if we are to improve the education offered to poor Latino and black students. Lower class sizes may help, as well as parental involvement, support, cooperation, and an emphasis on home-work and study (Howell and Peterson 2002). However, parents who are properly preparing their children for the school experience not only are more likely to be involved but are also more likely to be supportive and cooperative. Their efforts allow the school-related variables to become relevant.

This research builds upon the work of others who have stressed the role of the family of poor black and poor Latino students in the education of those students, and suggests that we need to begin to look beyond schools in our efforts to bridge the performance gap. Public schools are middle-class institutions, and we should not therefore be surprised to learn that middle-class students do better than others. The truth is, however, that some poor students are, in fact, middle class, and all other things being equal (which they seldom are), will do well in school. They do not have middle incomes, and their parents do not have the education or the occupations that place them among the middle-income/class, but the parents have the values, beliefs, expectations, and often the school-related behaviors that place them there.

They have the high expectations, the belief in discipline and respon-sibility, the understanding of the value of delayed gratification and internal control, the absolute requirement that their children will do their schoolwork (and their responsibility to help them with the work), and an insistence upon a quiet and orderly environment in which the students may do that work. These parents know the value of high self-esteem in their children and the importance of clear and consistent role boundaries. In other words, they are in many ways as critially important to schools as middle-class parents, but without the middle incomes. This is not easy to maintain, but a number of poor Latino and poor black parents manage to do it, and we observe some of them in this work. We also observe some who do not, and we compare and contrast the black and Latino parents, as well as revisit five poor black families we observed several years ago to find out whether their family patterns and the students' grades have changed over time.

This work requires a great deal of dedication and effort, given that we spend a fair amount of time in the homes of a number of poor families. I would like to thank those families for allowing us into their homes for weeks. I would also like to thank Ms. Joanne Avery and Mr. Theodore Haynes, who served as research assistants. Ms. Avery, a staff member at Family Focus, the community-based agency that made this work possible, was great.

A number of students at DePaul University also made this project successful: Ricardo Acosta, Saria Amjad, Emily Baldauf, Julie Barki, Suzee Bending, Andrew Born, Linda Brooks, Ceilia Ceja, Julie Courtney, Manuela Dela Cruz, Christina DeLarosa, Jonathan Diaz, Ben Douglas, Michelle Duff, Laurel Eby, Amber Foster, Laurie Grauer, Elizabeth Hale, Ian Hall, Nora Johnson, Matt Kitson, Katherine Kost, Esmeralda Martinez, Kimberely Maxwell, James Muhammed, Natasha Najar, Charles Patton, Jonathon Pierce, Felicia Ramos, Ryan Robertson, Steven Simon, Juana Telles, Mike Urbanus, and Anthony Voit.

Finally, I would like to challenge William M. Dobbs, another young black student, to take this work and his life to another, a higher, level.

①

SCHOOL PREPARATION
AMONG THE DISADVANTAGED

According to Valdes (1998), the study of the family unit is critical in understanding the academic achievement of Mexican immigrant children. Irvine (1991) argues that for black parents, their role as teachers in the home is "crucial," and is the one role directly related to the achievement of black students. Ogbu (2003, 241) writes, "parents' supervision of their schoolwork and homework was an important reason for their academic success," according to black students he studied who were doing well in school. Yet the teachers of these students tended to believe that poor and working-class black parents fail to supervise the homework of their children. We know that black and Latino children living in poverty are far more likely than others to have academic difficulties, "including low performance on cognitive tests, low school performance, and higher rates of school drop out than their nonpoor European-American peers" (Gutman and McLoyd 2000, 2; see also Valdes 1998).

Despite the continued low academic performance of poor Latino and poor black students, for the most part, those concerned with this situation continue to look to schools for school-based solutions and fail to pay sufficient attention to the family as a possible source of help. As Gutman and McLoyd put it, "Research on the family life of poor African-American children, however, is miniscule"—this despite the fact "that the home is the major ecological setting for children" (Gutman and McLoyd 2000, 3). Or, as Tapia (2000, 26) puts it with respect to Mexican Americans, "I argue that Mexican-American students' learning and academic achievement can be better understood by taking the household as the unit of analysis and by following family members' school-derived activities through time."

Recently, a number of scholars (including Furstenberg et al. 1999; Bempechat 1998; Ogbu 2003; Sampson 2002, 2003; Valdes 1998; and Tapia 2000) have built upon the earlier work of Clark (1983), which focused upon the family as the key unit for school preparation and learning for poor black students (in Clark's case) and for poor Latino students or poor students in general in some of the other works. Still, very little research dealing with the academic performance of poor nonwhite students examines the role of the family in the educational process. I believe that this is a grave mistake, given the poor performance of poor black and Latino students in school.

Educational attainment for Latinos is quite low (Baron and Vasquez 1990). This is the case whether we look at reading, vocabulary, or math (Valdes 1998). As for black students, they trail white students significantly in grade point average, course-level enrollment, and participation in gifted and special education programs (Ogbu 2003). Just what are we to do about this gap between Latino and black students on the one hand, and white students on the other? It is important to understand that my focus and concern is with the performance of poor Latinos and poor blacks, and I realize that not all Latinos or all blacks are poor. While middle-income blacks and Latinos also trail middle-income whites in academic performance, they are not my concern here, in part because most of them will manage to do fine both in school and in life. I am not looking for a way to bridge the "achievement gap" between whites and blacks and Latinos, but between poor blacks and poor Latinos with everyone else.

Despite the data showing what Howell and Peterson (2002) refer to as the "education gap," a number of poor black and poor Latino students do well in school. Why is that these students can do well despite poverty, language barriers, often inadequate funding of their schools, and high crime rates in their neighborhoods, while others in the same neighborhoods, with the same "limitations," and attending the same schools perform poorly? This is the central question that my research seeks to answer; the research upon which my work is based suggests that the answer lies with the family.

As Comer (1993, 303) puts it, "Development begins with the family. The family is enmeshed in and carries the attitudes, values, and ways of its social network." I submit that it is largely these attitudes, values, and ways that best determine just how well a child will perform in school, all other things being equal. Schools require discipline. Sitting in a hot classroom in the fall listening to a teacher talk about some person or place very far away and with apparently little relevance to you as a student requires discipline. Schools require high self-esteem. Most of us get a lot of answers wrong in school. If one cannot handle the corrections and criticism that come with that, one cannot handle school very well. Schools require us to be able to delay gratification. Most of us would rather be out playing on a warm spring day rather than sitting in a row of chairs listening to a teacher talk about Chaucer or Giovanni or Jorge Luis Borges—yet we put up with this because we believe that it will help us in the future. We, of course, must be able to conceptualize that future and to delay our current gratification.

"The school is an instrument of the mainstream culture" (Comer 1993, 305). Schools not only inculcate that middle-class–middle-income culture into our children but they are also designed, at least the public schools are, to shape and mold students to fit into that culture. Yet many poor families are not really a part of that culture; as a result, they send children to school ill prepared to learn. The children lack the values, attitudes, beliefs, and ways upon which the school is built, and which the school uses to teach the child. Such children are often hopelessly behind when they start school. If the parents fail to work to boost the self-esteem of the child, fail to teach the child to delay gratification, fail to teach the child discipline or the moral and intellectual-cognitive lessons so important in the school, not only does that child begin the educational experience behind but he or she is likely to fall even farther behind as the school experience becomes increasingly negative (Lightfoot 1978).

Still, this is not the case for all poor Latinos or poor blacks. As Gutman and McLoyd (2000) put it, "However, demographic circumstances are not an absolute predictor of individual success or failure. There are poor African-American children like Caryn, who experience academic success despite these tremendous odds" (2–3). The authors go on to write, "Although poor African-American youth often live in dangerous, violent neighborhoods (Wilson, 1987) and confront stark inequalities in terms of the quality of their school environments and educational opportunities (Kozol, 1990), other factors in their lives may help to sustain and nurture their academic development" (3). The most prominent of these "other factors" is the family, and while Gutman and McLoyd make this argument about poor blacks, Valdes make a similar argument about poor Latinos. The situation is even more difficult for many of them because of the language barrier, and what many see as cultural differences (Valdes 1998; Valencia 1991).

Much of the research on black families and achievement (or lack thereof) has utilized the "cultural deficit" model, which suggests that black families lack the exposure to mainstream culture, the parental value of education, and the necessary home environment for their children to perform well in school (Coleman et al. 1966; Jencks et al. 1972; Moynihan 1965). Although the "cultural deficit" or "culture of poverty" model developed before much serious research on the academic achievement of poor Latinos was conducted, the same model is used by some (Grossman 1995) to help explain the poor performance of many Latino students. In the case of Latinos, however, we must remember that many of them were indeed socialized into a different culture. This should not, however, be used as an excuse for the failure of our schools to properly educate their children, as has been the case for blacks.

"While much of the cultural deficit–oriented research and literature on Black families has concentrated on socioeconomic status (SES), marital and occupational status, family composition (particularly the absence of fathers in the home)—important variables to say the least— these factors do not fully explain achievement or underachievement among Blacks" (Ford 1993, 48), or among Latinos (Tapia 2000). Both Tapia and Ford go on to argue that the family is the best unit of analysis if one is to understand the academic achievement of poor Latino and poor black students, respectively.

Therefore, it makes sense to focus upon the family. However, I want to better understand why some poor Latino and poor black students can manage to do well, while others in the same schools and same neighborhood cannot. Further, I want to delve into the similarities and differences between poor Latinos and poor blacks in the same schools and, for the most part, the same neighborhood.

We would do well to remember that neither blacks nor Latinos are monolithic, and the same approaches to educating some Latinos or some blacks may not work well for others. Not all blacks are poor, and some poor blacks are in fact middle class in terms of their values, attitudes, and beliefs. All other things being equal, the children in these families tend to perform quite well in public schools, which are, after all, middle-class institutions. Some poor blacks and poor Latinos have discipline, ability to delay gratification, internal control, high self-esteem, sense of responsibility, and the ability to conceptualize and plan for a future—all characteristics needed for good performance in schools (Clark 1983; Ford 1993; Comer 1993).

All too often, scholars, teachers, and educational administrators look at all blacks and Latinos as though they are the same: disinterested, undisciplined, with no ability to delay gratification, and little sense of responsibility. Sometimes they chalk this up to poverty, as though all Latinos and blacks are poor. Other times they attribute this to race. Often, they see both as a problem, though they cannot get away with arguing that race is a "problem," so they chalk it up to "culture." In the case of blacks, this is really a camouflaged "cultural deficit" argument. In the case of Latinos, culture may indeed be a factor, depending upon how long the family has been in the United States and how acculturated they have become.

Irvine (1991) points out that some poor black students perform well in school while others perform poorly and attributes the difference to differences in the schools that the students attend. This is the "effective schools" argument, which suggests that some schools serving poor minority students are more effective than others, and then seeks to identify the characteristics of the effective schools so that other schools may copy these characteristics. Ron Edmonds (1979) has been the leader of this effort and body of research. Edmonds determined that effective schools had strong principals who functioned as instructional leaders, a focus on reading and math skills, frequent monitoring of student progress, and teachers with high expectations for the students (Irvine 1991).

On the surface, this school of thought seems to acknowledge differences among poor minority students. In reality, it lumps them together, and suggests that it is really differences among schools that are important, and that the schools that are less successful at educating poor minority students should emulate those that seem to do well. This argument (and much of the research upon which it is based) ignores the possibility of self-selection, and therefore ignores differences among poor minority students and their families. That is, it is very likely that those black families with essentially middle-class characteristics are the same ones who seek out certain schools, pressure the staff, and send their children to school prepared to learn. Of course, the students in these schools perform better than others, but is it the schools or the parents and their preparation of the children? It is likely the latter!

While I admire and make frequent reference to the work of Bempechat (1998), I believe that she makes the same mistake in dealing with the self-selection issue. She addresses the issue directly, and concludes, "I believe strongly that self selection—the notion that it is the higher-achieving students who are selecting Catholic over public education—is not as critical an issue as some have argued, nor as critical as it may have been at one time" (27). The focus here is upon Catholic schools because many of those located in poor minority neighborhoods seem to have students who perform better than their peers attending local public schools. She goes on to write, "Catholic schools do not pick and choose the best students available" (27). She does not seem to understand that the families who best prepare their students for school select the schools! No, the schools do not pick and choose, but the parents do. In fact, the parents who do the required homework, go through the necessary application process, and agree to the required participation are, by definition, a kind of parent different from others.

To do all of this, they must have a vision for their children, have discipline, be willing to sacrifice, be internally controlled, and in all likelihood, teach these characteristics to their children. I do not believe that Catholic schools have any magic formula for educating poor minority students, nor do I believe that some public schools are more effective than others because they have a special principal or staff or approach. This argument shortchanges the very same parents who, so many now argue, are crucial to the educational success of their children.

Most scholars and educators would agree that parents are critical to the educational process. However, for the most part, when parental participation is discussed, it is a form of "surface participation," or a very narrow and shallow definition of that participation. Irvine (1991) notes that most schools pay attention mainly to parental involvement in parent-teacher conferences, PTA meetings, and other school-based events and activities, or what Lightfoot (1978) refers to as "contrived occasions." It appears, however, that the more important form of parental participation is the direct involvement of the parents in the preparation of their children for school. Irvine suggests, "What appears to be a crucial role for black parents is their role as teachers in the home" (110). While I believe that Irvine makes a serious mistake by lumping all black parents together, her point is well taken. Gutman and McLoyd (2000) as well as Tapia (2000) and Ogbu (2003) make the same point: Parental supervision of and help with the child's homework are crucial to the academic success of the child.

In an earlier study of poor black students and their families, I found that parental involvement in homework was very important to the academic success of the student, even when the parent did not completely understand the homework (Sampson 2002). This suggests to me that it is less the actual help and answers offered by the parent, and more the message concerning both the importance of the work and the need for sacrifice and discipline that the involvement sends to the child that is most important. Parents working with their children, supervising their time, encouraging them, challenging them, and questioning them—these are the important issues here.

This does not imply that schools are not important to the educational process. Of course they are. If schools lack basic facilities, adequate learning materials, or trained and motivated teachers and administrators, they cannot do their jobs effectively no matter how well prepared the students. Indeed, as Gutman and McLoyd (2000) point out, it is a combination of home, school, and community that determines how well poor minority children will do in school. Ogbu (2003) suggests that it is "system factors"—a combination of societal and school factors—and "community forces" (which includes families) that determine how well poor minority children will do in school. Tapia (2000), writing about poor Mexican American students, suggests as well that school, home, and community influence the learning of poor Latinos.

Since the vast majority of the research on the performance of poor minority students has focused upon the school (Tapia 2000; Gutman and

McLoyd 2000) and much less often upon the impact of the family on achievement, we know relatively little about this role. While Clark (1983), Comer (1993), Valdes (1998), Tapia (2000), Bempechat (1998), Lareau (1989), Ford (1993), and several others have focused upon the family, the research concerning and discussion regarding the improvement of the education offered to poor nonwhites (beyond the surface participation or contrived occasions) continues to center upon schools, for the most part. The 1989 book by Slavin, Karweit, and Madden entitled *Effective Programs for Students at Risk* has not one chapter of the twelve dealing with the family. There is one paragraph dealing with a Family Support Team that they indicate should work with families to help involve parents in teaching their children to read, and to establish "opportunities for parents to volunteer within the school" (362), precisely the kind of surface participation that I believe has very little value in terms of preparing a student for school. Indeed, I suspect that those parents most likely to be involved in school-based activities are the same parents most likely to send their children to school prepared to learn, and are therefore not the parents who most need help.

The parents who feel comfortable in the school environment, who are able to work with middle-income, highly educated administrators and teachers in a very structured environment, are not the ones whose children are most likely to have problems. Other parents, however, who might well be intimidated by the school environment, nevertheless do what is needed at home. It is what they do and how they do it that are the focus of this work. This attempts to build upon the work of Clark (1983), Tapia (2000), Comer (1993), Ogbu (2003), and Sampson (2002, 2003), all of which examine the role played by the poor minority family in the preparation of their children for school. In this case, the families are all poor black and Latino families, living in the same neighborhood (which in itself is rare in America) in one large suburb of Chicago, and attending the same schools. I lay out the specific details about the families and the location in chapter 2 when I discuss the methodology.

According to Clark (1983), Ogbu (2003), Bempechat (1998), Tapia (2000), Valdes (1998), Sampson (2002 and 2003), and Comer (1993), the families of poor minority students who do well in school have a number of similarities: the stress placed upon discipline, the effort to see to it that the children have high self-esteem, the internal control, the ability to delay gratification, and high expectations. The parents in these homes also monitor the child's time fairly closely, for example, making certain that they do not watch a great deal of television, and that none is watched until homework is complete. The children are involved in extracurricular activities. This helps with discipline and helps the child to understand the value of structure in his or her life. The parents engage in learning activities with the child, activities such as reading and discussion of school-related topics. The parents tend to assign household chores to the children. This too helps with discipline and the development of a sense of responsibility.

In those families in which the children perform well in school, then, there is a lot of discipline, structure, talk, reading, support from parents, homework, chores, and involvement outside of the school and the home. While this is not an environment that is easy to maintain when one must worry about paying bills, drugs in the neighborhood, violence in the area, and others who do not share a dedication to the task of preparing children for school, a number of poor black and Latino parents nevertheless manage to do it. The task is even more difficult for some poor Latino families because many of the parents do not speak English, which severely limits their ability to interact with the school or to help the child with homework. In fact, it is often the child who helps the parent to negotiate the English-speaking world (Sampson 2003).

As Grossman (1995) and Sanchez (1997) point out, there are also likely to be cultural differences that make the educational process even more difficult and complicated for many poor Latino families. Many poor Latino families have tremendous respect both for authority and for teachers. This not only limits their propensity to challenge teachers or to discuss the education of their children with them but may well limit their involvement with the child in terms of helping with or supervising the homework because they believe that the teacher is always doing his or her job and the parents should not interfere. Then, too, it appears that in many poor Latino families the girls are raised to help the mother, to marry, and to have children. Tapia (2000) relates the household routine of one Mexican American family, "The routine was as follows: Ms. Rosales and Martha (the daughter) washed dishes and did other household chores. The routine involved Ms. Rosales getting the two boys started with homework and Martha's taking over this activity, allowing her mother to finish with household chores" (32). Martha was thirteen years old, yet she functioned to some extent as an extension of her mother, preparing for the role of mother, while the boys did their homework. The girls are not necessarily encouraged to pursue education. This would, of course, limit the motivation of the females.

According to Grossman (1995), "The Hispanic culture emphasizes learning by doing. As a result, some Hispanic students learn more by touching, seeing, manipulating and experiencing concrete objects than by discussing or reading about ideas" (82). Because reading and discussing are critical in the American educational system, this may well make performance in school more difficult for those Latino students who are more comfortable with an alternative style of learning. Many Latino parents, however, still manage to prepare their children for the educational experience and have children who perform well. They do many of the same things that I mentioned above as helping to lead to higher performance for poor minority students, and some manage this with limited English proficiency. Still, as we examine the roles played by poor black and Latino families in the preparation of the children for the educational experience, we would do well to remember that there may be cultural differences at play for the Latino families.

Most young people face pressure from their peers as they grow and develop. Indeed, the pressure to fit in is often intense. However, according to Ogbu (2003), black students (and according to Tapia [2000], some Latino students as well) face pressure from their peers that may well lead to poor school performance. Or as Ogbu puts it, "Peer pressure among Black American students is likely to be negative toward academic engagement for two reasons: First, as we noted in the last chapter, Blacks tend to interpret school curriculum and language as White impositions; they also experience the curriculum and language negatively because Americans have historically used both to communicate to black people that they are inferior" (189). He goes on to write, "Some researchers have noted that Black linguistic and behavioral responses appear to be a rejection of what they perceive as White people's attempt to define 'White ways' as the 'right ways' to talk and behave and 'Black ways' as the 'wrong ways'" (189).

While I believe that it is important to examine the possibility of peer pressure on young black and Latino students to perform poorly in school, I also believe that Ogbu and other scholars make a very big mistake by lumping all blacks and Latinos into one basket, including all poor blacks and Latinos. What Ogbu refers to as "White ways" are in reality "middle-class ways," not even "middle-income ways." Society has given poor folks, especially poor blacks and Latinos, a built-in excuse for failure: they are after all, "only" poor and nonwhite. As Ogbu (1978) and Ford (1993) point out, the cultural deficit model explains away the academic failure of poor blacks, and now poor Latinos, by blaming an "inadequate" culture, rather than holding the individual accountable for his or her failure or success. Thus, if one does poorly in school, it is not his or her fault; it is the culture, over which they have no real control.

The problem with this explanation is that not only is it misguided but that it also only works if almost all of the members of the group perform poorly. If some poor blacks and poor Latinos do well in school, then why can't others? So, if you are a poor black or Latino student doing poorly and blaming variables other than yourself for that performance, you need others like yourself to also do poorly. You may therefore pressure those who would do well to lessen their performance in order to explain your own lack of performance.

Ford (2000) correctly points out that the cultural deficit model denies the differences among blacks, and I would add, the differences among Latinos. Many poor Latinos and poor blacks are middle class in terms of their attitudes, values, and beliefs; in public schools that are middle-class institutions, all other things being equal, their children are likely to do well. I am not dealing here only with the value of education in a family, which is the value about which much is written when scholars consider education, class, and values. As Ford (1993) correctly points out, almost all parents—black, white, poor, Latino, and middle income—say that they value education highly. No, I am concerned here with values such as discipline, self-control, and achievement—values that are essential to good school performance.

Some poor families seem to possess these values while others do not. My point here is that social class is not as cut-and-dried as many seem to believe, and this complexity has a profound impact upon the education of poor nonwhites. Lareau (2000), in her excellent (if limited) work, writes, "Social class has a powerful influence on parent involvement patterns. For example, between forty to sixty percent of working class and lower class parents fail to attend parent-teacher conferences. For middle class parents these figures are nearly halved" (3). She goes on to point out that parental involvement in school preparation activities such as "promoting verbal development, reading to children, taking children to the library, attending school events, enrolling children in summer school, and making complaints to the principal" (3) are essentially middle-class activities in which the working- and lower-class parents are far less likely to participate.

I do not believe that attending school events and complaining to principals are very important forms of participation, though I understand that educators think that they are. I am far more concerned with teaching children to read, helping with homework, supervising their activities, raising their self-esteem, promoting their independence and discipline, encouraging their participation in extracurricular activities, and teaching them to delay gratification than with whether parents attend a school-sponsored dinner, though attendance may well be an indicator that parents are indeed doing many of the things that I consider more important to the child's academic development and performance.

These activities are not, however, limited to the middle income, as Ogbu (2003) and Lareau (2000) appear to define that term. While Lareau writes about the middle and working classes, she is really referring to the middle- and lower-middle income groups, for class cannot be defined only by education, occupation, and income. As Furstenberg et al. (1999) and Harrington and Boardman (1997) point out, poor folks get out of poverty every day. The vast majority of them, I submit, are able to do so because they are essentially middle-class folks in terms of their values, beliefs and, attitudes and, given the opportunity, will use these values and beliefs to take advantage of the middle-class school system to rise out of poverty.

My point is that some poor blacks and poor Latinos appear to be middle class and do many of the things that seem to be important for good academic performance for their children, while others are not and do not. Why some and not others is beyond the scope of this research. This work, however, seeks to determine the veracity of this argument, to examine the family dynamic of poor black and poor Latino families as that dynamic relates to school performance of children in those families, and to compare and contrast the things done in poor black and poor Latino families as those things relate to school performance and the family preparation for that performance.

This work seeks to build upon and extend the work of scholars such as Clark (1983), Ogbu (2003), Tapia (2000), Gutman and McLoyd (2000), Valdes (1998), Lareau (2000), Sampson (2002, 2003), and Bempechat (1998). For the most part, these scholars studied poor black or poor Latino families to determine just how they worked to influence the academic performance of the children in those families. Lareau studied middle-income and lower middle-income white families (twelve of them), while Clark studied ten poor black families (and found half of them to be middle class). Tapia studied five Latino families, though he reports on only four of them, and made no attempt to control for income. Valdes focused upon three classrooms that were economically diverse at one middle school, but studied three Latino students. Ogbu studied the black community of Shaker Heights, Ohio, a relatively affluent suburb of Cleveland, and did not focus on specific families. Gutman and McLoyd studied a larger (N=62) number of poor black families.

Only Bempechat studied a multiethnic group of families, which is one of the things that I seek to do. In addition, I had observers monitor the children, all now high school students, in five of the twelve poor black families that I studied three years ago (Sampson 2002) to determine whether the things we saw several years ago were holding true today. In other words, I revisited almost half of the poor black families studied three years ago to see whether the home environment remained the same and how the students were doing in school a few years later— whether the positives remained and the negatives might have been turned around.

2

RESEARCH METHODS:
THE EVANSTON STUDY

Ford (1993), in discussing the need for more research on the role played by black families in the academic lives of their children, calls for a "new agenda," an "ecological approach" that "observes parental and child behavior within the environment in which it occurs and analyzes behavior according to the value systems of a family's indigenous culture or subculture." She is correct when she writes, "previous studies (particularly those conducted in the 1960s and 1970s—which are heavily referenced even today) tell us little about what happens educationally in the homes of Black children" (59). Tapia (2000) makes a similar argument regarding the need to focus research upon what he refers to as "the household" in Latino communities over time.

If one wishes to learn about what parents do and do not do that influences how children perform in school, then one needs to study in some detail the family lives of the parents and students. That is precisely what I have attempted to do here. Others—most notably Clark (1983), Furstenberg (1999), Tapia (2000), Ogbu (2003), Lareau (2000), and Bempechat (1998)—have studied the role of the family in the academic lives of minority children. With few exceptions, their work has utilized questionnaires to collect data about the lives of the families studied. The previous work, which has been invaluable in shaping and informing this work, has been ethnographic, and in the case of Ogbu's work (2003), observational as well.

Valdes (1998) studied four Mexican American students and their families and collected data using questionnaires with the parents, students, and school administrators, and classroom observations. She did not really observe the family or the "household." I believe that it is important to collect data from students and parents if one wishes to learn about family life and academic achievement. However, I also think that it is very important to observe the family dynamic over some time if one wishes to learn what parents do and do not do that influences the academic performance of their children. Questionnaires provide very important ethnographic data, but observations allow a close look at what really happens on a day-to-day basis in the family. Accordingly, I have used a combination of interviews and observations to collect the data for this study.

Both students and a parent (usually the mother) were interviewed, and observers monitored what went on in the homes on a daily basis on at least three occasions, and in most cases, four to five occasions. The observers were undergraduate students enrolled in a course at DePaul University entitled "Urban Poverty." A number of the students had taken previous courses from me and were, in a sense, selected for this course. The first two weeks of the course were devoted to training the observers to observe the poor families assigned to them and to taking field notes. One student who had been an observer in the past helped with this training.

As Lareau (2000) writes, "it is wise to have research projects that are intensive and small in scope. It is very difficult to mentally review and assess any more than fifty interviews." She also correctly notes that since "subjects need time to become accustomed to the presence of the interviewer/observer, multiple observations are required." Clark (1983) observed the ten families that he studied two times, during which he interviewed family members. Tapia (2000) observed the five families he studied over a three-year period, visiting the four households for which he reports data "from 15 to 23 times." It is obviously desirable to observe the family in its environment as many times as possible for as long as possible. However, if one wishes to observe a larger group of families, there are serious cost and time implications.

In the case of this research, I believe that it was unwise for me to be the observer, given that I had not only lived in the community that was the focus of the study for some twenty years, served on the school board at the schools attended by most of the students studied, and have a former relative who teaches in the middle school attended by many of the students, the same school attended by my two daughters.

Many poor families have reasons to be suspicious of folks they do not know well. Some have things that they believe that they need to hide from others. It is better in some sense for someone from the "outside" to make the observations, given that that someone is unlikely to be in a position to tell anyone from the community anything that may hurt those observed. In any event, given that we observed seventeen families, and focused upon twenty-two children in those seventeen families, it would have taken an enormous amount of time to collect all of the data were one person to perform the observations.

I had earlier studied twelve poor black families (Sampson 2002) and eight poor Latino families (Sampson 2003) in attempts to learn more about the role of poor nonwhite families and school preparation. Now I wanted to study a larger group of families in an effort to build the database and to check the validity of not only my previous findings but also those of other scholars such as Clark (1983), Bempechat (1998), Tapia (2000), Lareau (2000), Ogbu (2003), and Furstenberg (1999). Given that the methodology employed to some degree requires relatively small samples, we need repeated studies of these small samples in order to have confidence in the findings.

THE SAMPLE

All seventeen of the families studied live in Evanston, a diverse community of 74,239 people just north of Chicago. Latinos are 6.1 percent of the population, while blacks make up 22.5 percent of the population. Both blacks and Latinos are concentrated on the west side of the community (though a sizable number of Latinos also live in the southern part of town). Increasingly, the Latino population has moved into the section, which was historically black, and some 15 percent of both the black and Latino populations are below the poverty line.

Given that the research method utilized here is very invasive, requiring observers to be in homes for hours at a time on a number of occasions, it was critical that we have the trust of the families studied. I have learned from previous experience that it is best to work with a trusted community-based agency to gain access to the families. As in my previous work, the agency was Family Focus, a highly regarded community-based social service agency located in the heart of the community in which the vast majority of the observed families live.

Another Family Focus office that is located south of the one with which I worked this time helped with my previous work with poor Latinos. The main Family Focus facility has for years worked almost exclusively with poor black families and children, which makes sense given their location in the heart of the black community. However, as the Latino population has grown in that same community, the agency has adapted to accommodate the growing poor Latino population as well.

Evanston was selected both because the agency was willing to help and because it has a sizable population of poor blacks and a growing population of poor and working-class Latinos; Evanston also has a limited number of schools (four middle schools and one high school), so that differences in schools are unlikely to account for much difference in the performance of the students. This allows us to pay more attention to families than to schools. Indeed, the bulk of the students observed attend the local elementary and the local middle school, though several of the Latino students observed attend a different middle school. All of those five students whom we followed up from four years ago attend the community high school, Evanston Township High School.

Since we wanted to relate academic performance to that which does or does not occur in the home, we needed a measure of performance. In this case, we used the school grades of the students. However, Evanston does not give letter grades until the sixth grade, using teacher comments and indications of whether a student meets grade standards for the elementary grades. This makes comparisons of performance a bit more difficult for elementary school students. For this reason, we wanted to focus upon middle school students but, for a variety of reasons, younger students were also included in this research. These students were either fourth or fifth graders, just below middle school.

DATA COLLECTION AND LIMITATIONS

After the Family Focus staff approached a number of poor Latino and poor black families about their possible participation in the research, the observers and I were invited to a community dinner at the agency at which the work was discussed further, and observers were assigned to families by Family Focus staff members based largely upon what they knew about the families and the observers. For the most part, only Spanish-speaking observers were assigned to the Latino families. In fact, only one of the observers of these families was Anglo.

At the community dinner, each observer who was assigned a family wrote down the names and phone number of the family members and made their first appointment. At the same dinner, the staff member with whom we worked most closely suggested that we might want to consider following up on the twelve poor black families studied three years earlier to see just how those students were doing. Given that I had considered this myself (though in fairness, I must give the credit to the staff member), I jumped at the chance, and assigned observers to the families of the nine students who were still in Evanston. Only seven of the nine could be contacted, and five agreed to the observations and to answer the questions.

The observers had been trained to observe everything about family life, including interactions, interventions, values, attitudes, and responsibilities, and were to make these observations after school. We wanted to see the extent to which, for example, the parents helped with homework, encouraged the child, monitored the child's time and activities, encouraged independent thinking, assigned household chores, encouraged and supported participation in extracurricular activates, and maintained discipline and structure—in other words, what went on in the homes that was related to those characteristics of high-performing students: discipline, high self-esteem, ability to cooperate, internal control, high educational aspirations, the ability to delay gratification, and an orderly and structured home environment (Sampson 2002, 2003; Comer 1993; Clark 1983; Gutman and McLoyd 2000).

The observers were specifically taught not to interpret, just to observe, and they met once a week to discuss the experiences and observations, and to go over any problems encountered. I went over the observations weekly to note any glaring weaknesses or omissions, and then discussed any such problems with the observers. The names of all of the students and parents involved in this research have been changed to protect their identities. In some cases, the participants suggested the names by which they wanted to be known, but when they did not, either the observer or the analyst made the changes.

The sample is designed to allow direct comparisons between poor blacks and poor Latino families in the school preparation process in order to begin to examine the role played by race/ethnicity in the process for poor nonwhites. We observed six Latino students and sixteen black students. Thus far, almost all of the research on school preparation and involvement of poor families has centered on poor blacks, with a few pieces of research on Latinos (Valdes 1998; Delgado-Gaitan 1992; Tapia 2000), Lareau's work on poor and middle-income whites (2000), and Bempechat's work on "poor and minority" students (1998) deviating from this focus, and adding much-needed depth to this body of work.

My previous work on poor Latinos and school preparation (Sampson 2003) had only a poor Latino sample and used data from an earlier study of poor blacks (Sampson 2002) to make some comparisons. The comparisons were difficult and somewhat problematic because the sample of black families focused only upon middle school students, while the Latino sample was heavily made up of preschoolers. Of course, the preparation of preschoolers for school is quite different from the process of preparing older children for and supporting them in the educational experience. Furthermore, the two samples were drawn from somewhat different neighborhoods, meaning that neighborhood differences could affect the results. While this is unlikely given the size of the Evanston community, and the relatively few schools in the district, it is still a possibility that I wanted to limit in the present research.

While I believe that the ethnographic-observational technique is best suited to the research questions that are the focus of this work, the method is not without its weaknesses and limitations. In pointing out the limitations of her own quantitative research on black student achievement orientation and the family, Ford (1993) notes, "Clearly, there is much to learn from ethnographic studies that seek to determine phenomena without reification or quantification. Once researchers and educators delve beneath the surface of quantitative analyses, the dynamics of achievement among racially and culturally different groups may be more fully understood" (61–62).

Still, when one seeks to observe poor families over time, things do not always go as planned. Poor people have better things to do and more to worry about than keeping an appointment with a stranger who wants to watch what they do and listen to what they say. There are bill collectors to deal with, jobs to apply for, drugs in the neighborhood, and high crime rates; teachers who dress well and are well spoken may intimidate them. As a result, appointments are missed and questionnaires may not get filled out.

In five cases, two observers were assigned to the same family, but to observe two different children. I have learned from experience that it is rather difficult to focus upon the activities, thoughts, and words of more than one child at a time. This does, however, raise the possibility that we will see different academic performances from the different children in the same home, complicating the analysis. On the other hand, this allows us the opportunity to examine the possibility that different children in the same family are being prepared differently for the educational experience. In the small but growing research on the family's role in school preparation, this is rather new. The previous work, including my own with poor black families, has focused upon one student per family. While my work on poor Latino families (Sampson 2003) did examine more than one child per family, I did not have the grades of the children, which would have allowed comparisons of the academic achievement of siblings, and therefore of the impact of any differences in school preparation upon actual performance. This work allows those comparisons, and brings into play issues such as gender differences within the family, as well as birth order differences. This, of course, assumes no large family differences in intelligence, but does not take for granted personality differences.

The relatively small size of the Evanston elementary and middle school system limits the variation among schools and therefore reduces the chance that variation in schools will influence the findings in a significant way. However, the size and suburban location also limits the generalizability of the findings, as does the relatively large, but statistically small, sample. More ethnographic research relating the family dynamic to the academic achievement of students is sorely needed, and we need to determine whether the size, location, or diversity of the community makes any difference. I have seen almost no work on rural locations, for example. The current work seeks to add to our base of knowledge. However, I also pay no attention to school factors that might affect the performance of poor black and poor Latino students. This does not mean that these factors are not important. Because almost all of the work that deals with the academic performance of poor minority students centers upon school factors, and because we still have not changed those factors in a way that has made a significant difference in the performance of any significant number of these students, a different focus would appear to be in order.

Finally, Gerald Graff in his latest work (2003) cautions against the idea that the academic world must be "impenetrable," using arcane language, and separate itself from the rest of the world. An old professor of mine once told me that the average number of readers of an academic article is seven, and that includes the outside reviewers and the spouse of the author! This work is aimed not only at education scholars and those academicians concerned with the topics of race, ethnicity, and social class but also at educational policymakers, social service workers working with students, teachers, and even parents. It is therefore written in a way to which all can relate. This lack of obfuscation may not sit well with some of my academic colleagues but I believe that the topic is too important to be the subject of only academic discussion.

3

FAMILY ANALYSIS FOR MULTIPLE-STUDENT FAMILIES

There is little doubt that black students and Latino students, as groups, have relatively low rates of educational achievement, and this is particularly the case for poor Latinos and poor blacks. Irvine (1991) attributes the difference to race, social class, and culture. Lareau (2000) points to social class as it limits parental involvement and therefore academic achievement. Ogbu (2003) stresses "academic disengagement" as a primary cause. All three of these authors studied black students and black families. I have my doubts about the culture argument, because it is not clear to me that there is one "black culture." I also believe that the social class argument as presented by these and other scholars is off base, primarily because it uses a very limited definition of class, and thereby fails to consider that the variables most closely linked to performance are not necessarily closely linked to education, occupation, and income, the variables usually used to define and measure social class.

I believe that the culture argument is stronger for many Latino families, who often come from and maintain a culture quite different from that seen in much of the United States and therefore different from the backbone of most public education. Further, many of these families also face problems with language. However, the point here is that poor Latino and poor black students tend to perform poorly in the classroom.

Although I may disagree with some scholars on the explanations for this performance, there is no disagreement about the overall performance—yet that is not the case for a number of the poor black and poor Latino students observed for this research.

It should be pointed out that the definition of success varies from scholar to scholar but is central to any analysis of the academic achievement of poor minority students. Clark (1983) does not offer any precise definition of academic success, and it appears that he considered students who were in fact average as "high achievers." He relied upon the reports of students for the grades. Tapia (2000) appears to classify those students earning As and Bs as high achievers, and the source of the grades is unclear. Lareau (2000) does not use specific grades much in her analysis. Given the obstacles faced by poor black and poor Latino students, should we use definitions for achievement different from those that might be used for middle-income Anglo students? I think not. Given that all of these students must compete against each other for college positions, jobs, and positions in life, it makes sense to me to use the same definitions. The problem is that there is no one standard definition of academic achievement.

I have classified average achievement as earning mostly grades of C or "Meets Grade-level Standards" for those not yet in middle school in Evanston. Given this definition, three of the twenty-two students observed are above average in academic achievement, twelve are average, and seven are below average. This, of course, does not include the five students who were observed for the second time. While I was somewhat surprised that only three students were above average, I suspect that some folks will be surprised that such a large percentage of the poor minority students are doing fairly well academically. It is certainly not the case that this is a group of poor black and Latino students who are failing academically. For the most part they are doing fairly well, and Ashley Knowles, Raven Johnson, and Angela King are doing quite well.[*]

In my previous work with poor black families (Sampson 2002), the analysis was arranged and done by achievement level of the student.

---

[*] The names of the students have been changed to help to protect their privacy, and the students were asked to select a name for themselves and their family. If they did not make a selection, I did this for them.

However, in this case, in which we observed two students in each of five families and we can compare the academic performance of those students within the family, it makes more sense to perform the analysis by family. This allows the reader to follow the analysis more easily. Were the analysis done by academic performance level, the reader would read the analysis of the family preparation for one student in the family and then not see the analysis for the other for perhaps many pages, if there were a difference in the performance level of the siblings. For this reason, the first data presentation chapter will be by family, and the next three will be by student academic achievement level.

THE KNOWLES FAMILY

Ashley Knowles attends the middle school that serves the bulk of the poor black and Latino students on the west side of Evanston; she is an eleven-year-old sixth grader. In the latest grading period, she received two grades of A, two grades of B, and two grades of C. By almost any measure, she is an above-average student. Her mother, Ms. Knowles, is a single parent, and there are seven children in her household. She lives in the neighborhood on the west side in which the majority of poor black and poor Latinos in Evanston live, and has lived in Evanston for over thirty-five years. Ms. Knowles works at a hospital full time and has completed three years of trade school. She believes that Ashley's education is "very, very important" to her because she wants "my kids to go to school and be more successful than I was" and because "School is also very important to succeed in life and getting a good job."

She says that she encourages her children to read a book for at least thirty minutes a day, and points out that school "will keep you off the corners." She says that she visits Ashley's school twelve to fifteen times a year, which seems like quite a few visits, and suggests that she is very much involved in Ashley's education, and not "disengaged," as Ogbu (2003) might put it. When she visits the school, she feels "very concerned, very worried" and notes that there is "no communication." As Comer (1993) notes, schools are middle-class institutions, and the attitude and presentation of the teachers and administrators may well be off-putting to some poor, not well-educated parents, causing communication problems, and complicating the educational process. Teachers and administrators may do well to remember this.

Ms. Knowles believes that nothing stands in the way of her daughter's receiving a good education, suggesting that she expects Ashley to do well, and that she does not look to others or other variables to determine her daughter's educational success. She does not believe that other children or adults at Ashley's school stand in her way or try to hinder her success, nor does she believe that racial discrimination plays a role in her life. The idea that other students try to limit the academic success of some poor minority children as a way of justifying their own lack of success, while appealing in some ways, is an idea for which I have not found much empirical support. I have indicated in my previous work that I think that it makes some sense, but I have yet to find much support for it in my data.

In raising Ashley and her siblings, Ms. Knowles says that she stresses self-control and discipline, and talks to them about their future. She also focuses upon the job market and points them in the direction of careers that may be available. Of course, discipline and self-control are two of the most important characteristics of students who do well in school (Clark 1983; Sampson 2002, 2003; Furstenberg et al. 1999).

When asked what she most likes about school, Ashley responded, "Friends, gym, art, reading," and she most dislikes the teachers, an interesting response for a student doing well. She believes that she is doing well as opposed to "Very Well, Pretty Good, Not So Well, or Poorly." She thinks that her education is important because she likes learning different things, and she indicates that no one has ever tried to stop her from doing well in school. She says that she devotes forty-five minutes per day to her homework, and that she would like to go to college. Indeed, she expects to go to college, suggesting high educational expectations on her part, and sees no obstacles in her way. Remember, this is an eleven-year-old poor black student being raised by her mother in a poor neighborhood with six other children in the home. Her race, socioeconomic status, and marital status of her mother have not appeared to affect her educational expectations or sense of efficacy. As Ford (1993) points out, this is often the case despite what many in the public and the supporters of the cultural deficit model seem to believe.

Ashley thinks that school and family are the most important things in her life, and she feels close to a particular sixth-grade teacher who is "really nice and not that hard and does not give much homework." If she could be anyone in the world, she would be Beyonce, "because she is rich and because she can sing and dance." So, while she has high education expectations and aspirations, like many young girls she would like to be the glamorous star if she had the chance.

Like Ford (1993), Clark (1983), Comer (1993), Tapia (2000), Ogbu (2003), and Furstenberg et al. (1999), I believe that the values, beliefs, and attitudes of a family have a profound impact upon educational performance, and that these values, attitudes, and beliefs, while affected by income, occupation, education, race, and ethnicity, are not determined by them. That is, poor black and Latino families often maintain the values and beliefs most helpful for the educational success of their children. If not hindered by inadequate teachers, administrators, or facilities (which is unfortunately often the case), they can impart these values, attitudes, and beliefs to their children and watch them do well in school. While the answers to the questions posed in the questionnaires to Ashley and her mother suggest that several of the needed values, attitudes, and beliefs are present, it is the data collected through the observations that should be most illuminating.

Ashley lives in a two-unit building that is spacious but without much furniture. Ms. Knowles's brother lives with her family, along with the seven children. During the first visit, Ashley did no schoolwork or household chores, and her mother pointed out to the observer that she believed that the problem with the education given to her children was that the teachers did not believe that the parents cared about the education of their children. In fact, most of the time during the first visit was devoted to a discussion of this topic and to Ashley asking the observer questions about her. This would not be unusual for a young girl who may well have had little attention paid to her in the past. But the discussion with Ms. Knowles suggests that she believes that teachers have low expectations of poor minority parents, which adversely affects their teaching of the children. Not a new idea, but it does indicate that Ms. Knowles is not only paying attention to the education of her daughter but analyzing it as well.

During the second visit, Ashley pointed out that she had done better on her math exam, and talked about a fight she had witnessed. She then went to the kitchen to get a snack prior to dinner. She, a brother, and the observers then played checkers until the dinner (pizza) arrived. While eating, the observers and the students discussed sports, and they cleaned up after dinner.

The next time, the observer arrived before Ms. Knowles arrived from work. This visit took place on a Wednesday, unlike the previous visits, which took place on Fridays. The difference is important, given that young students may well alter their routine on the weekend. When Ms. Knowles arrived from work, she asked right away whether Ashley had completed her homework. Ashley cleared the table and began to work on her math and then her history, with her uncle helping her with the work. She devoted forty-five minutes to the math, and then fifteen minutes to the history. So, we see that Ms. Knowles asked about schoolwork, Ashley did her work, and that her uncle helped her. Help with schoolwork is important not only because of the expertise offered but because it sends a message to the student about the importance of the work to the adults in the home. If they will take the time from their schedules to help with the work, then it must be important.

During the next visit, Ashley pointed out that she would have made the honor role were it not for her two Cs. This suggests how important both school and achievement are to her. While her brother appeared "proud" of his grades, Ms. Knowles was not happy with them. She seems to expect high performances from both children. The evening was spent watching a movie. During the next visit, Ashley's uncle asked both she and her brother about their homework. Although they both replied that they did have work to do, neither made any effort to do the work, with Ashley spending her time with her CDs, and then playing chess with her brother, before going to her aunt's house.

Although Ashley receives above-average grades, the family does not seem to exhibit a number of the characteristics of the families of high-achieving students. Her mother talks about discipline being important, but we saw little attempt to enforce discipline with Ashley. Both Ashley and her mother seem to have high educational expectations, yet we saw her do little schoolwork at home. We saw no involvement in household chores that stress discipline and responsibility, and no involvement in extracurricular activities, which emphasizes positive self-esteem, discipline, and responsibility, all of which are important to educational success. Ashley did not appear to delay gratification very much, getting her snacks before dinner when she wanted to do so, and playing with her CDs rather than doing her homework. Her teachers, however, see little problem with her behavior or work habits in the classroom.

The same cannot be said for her twelve-year-old brother, James, who is a seventh grader at the same school attended by Ashley. For the last grading period, James received one B, three Cs (in music, art, and physical education), two Ds, and one F. So, in the academic areas he had two Ds, a B, and an F, suggesting a below-average performance. Further, several teachers indicate that he does not make good use of his class time, one suggests that he is poorly organized, while another reports that he does not work independently.

Thus, while Ashley is above average in the classroom, her brother James, raised in the same house by the same single mother, and less than two years older than Ashley, is below average. Why? Well, Ms. Knowles calls James "very delayed" and "lazy," and indicates that she does not understand the lack of help from teachers.

For his part, when asked what he most likes about school, James answered, "the principal" and "gym," and he least likes "the teachers." Curiously, James believes that he is doing well in school, despite the obviously low grades. Like his sister, James says that education is "very important" to him, because it will allow him to avoid "messed-up" jobs. Both of the Knowles children link education very closely with jobs. James, too, expects to go to college, and believes that there are no obstacles in his way. He reports spending about an hour a day on his homework. To him, family, money, and education are the most important things in his life, and he would change nothing about his family life. His mother helps "a lot" with his homework, but we saw no such help with Ashley. He would be Bill Gates if he could be any one person in the world because "he is the richest man." He appears to be more focused upon money than education, and education seems be a way to that money in his view.

During the first visit to James's house, the observer noted (as did the observer assigned to Ashley) that the home was very sparsely furnished. James was at home with three brothers, Ashley, and a cousin. When Ms. Knowles arrived home, she began a discussion with the observers about the poor academic performance of some students. She attributes this poor performance to the failure of teachers to listen to parents, and noted that the teachers talk with her in an arrogant manner. She expressed concern that students were promoted to the next grade without adequate knowledge of subject matter, and pointed out that this social promotion will hurt them in high school and college.

While this conversation took place, James played board games with Ashley, and there was no homework done. The conversation with Ms. Knowles is interesting. She clearly is paying attention to some of the educational issues confronting many poor black students: the failure of many teachers to adequately communicate with parents (and the failure of many parents to even care) and the issue of social promotion. She appears to take a fairly hard stance on these issues, but the fact that she is thinking about them and has a position suggests her concern about the education of her children. On the other hand, James did no homework or household chores, and did not appear to be involved in any extracurricular activities, all of which are associated with higher academic achievement. Nor did Ms. Knowles show any effort to raise the self-esteem of either child or to impose discipline.

During the next visit, the observer noticed that the dining room was now fully furnished. This time James and Ashley played checkers, laughing and joking with each other during the game. Ms. Knowles had ordered pizzas for dinner, which arrived while the observers, at the suggestion of the students, played various games themselves. Again, there was no homework done. After eating, James did clear the table of the paper plates and plastic cups that were used for dinner.

During the five visits to the Knowles home, James was never seen doing homework, spending most of his time playing various games, watching videos, and snacking, despite the fact that his mother was in the home every time. She did not ask about school or homework, nor did she monitor his activities. There were really none of the characteristics of the homes of higher-achieving students: discipline; internal control; responsibility; high self-esteem; an orderly, structured environment; parental involvement in the intellectual activities of the student; and delayed gratification. The two siblings did seem to cooperate with each other, and a spirit of cooperation is a characteristic of the homes of higher-achieving students. While there was little disruption in the home, the environment did not appear to be centered on the academic lives of the two students. Indeed, very little attention was paid to this at all. It is then somewhat surprising that Ashley is doing as well as she is in school, and no surprise that James is not doing well. Ms. Knowles, for all of her expressed concern about education, has not apparently managed to translate the concern into the kinds of behaviors and activities that help to prepare the students for academic success.

Still, one child is doing well while the other is performing poorly in school, despite being raised in the same home environment, attending the same school, and being just over a year apart in age. It may be that Ashley has greater motivation than James; although we saw no clear indication of this in our observations, it is nevertheless a possibility. This is an issue to bear in mind as we proceed with the data presentation and analysis of families with more than one student observed. It is the case, however, that the family has recently experienced very serious financial problems that have perhaps affected James more than they have Ashley.

THE LOVES

Raven Love is an eleven-year-old sixth grader at the same middle school attended by the Knowles siblings. Her grades, like Ashley's, are above average. In the fall grading period, she received two grades of B and three Cs. However, in three of her classes, her teachers considered her behavior and/or work habits to be inconsistent, expressing concern about her self-control and ability to work cooperatively.

Raven lives with her mother, her mother's husband, and her brother, Andrew, who is twelve years old. Ms. Love has lived in Evanston for one year, is thirty-two years old, and completed the tenth grade in school. Her husband, a taxi driver, is from Africa and has a GED. She says that Raven's education is "very vital" to her because "[Raven] needs a fighting chance in the world. She is female and black." She emphatically states that she tries to help Raven to do well in school, and does this by "setting goals" and by "improving their living quarters." She visits her daughter's school "sometimes once a week," and says that she feels "very angry and disappointed" when she does so. According to Ms. Love, the teachers at the school do not respect the parents or the children and "are not in the right mind-set." This is much like the complaint offered by Ms. Knowles, and suggests that perhaps some teachers are not sufficiently sensitive to their treatment of poor black parents or students. I have indicated before that it appears to be the case that students sent to school prepared to learn will do well, all other things being equal. That is, if the teachers and administrators are properly trained, motivated, and sensitive, the facilities adequate, and the supplies in place, then students prepared by their parents to learn will do well, assuming no other obstacles. Well, both Ms. Love and Ms. Knowles apparently believe that all other things are not equal for their children. Still, Raven and Ashley manage to do well in the same school.

Ms. Love does indicate that other children sometimes try to stop Raven from doing well in school. There is an argument that some poor nonwhite students try to stop others from doing well in school because doing well is not expected of poor nonwhites, and this low expectation provides a kind of "cover" for those doing poorly (Sampson 2002). School success is then seen by some as "acting white" and is to be avoided (Fordham and Ogbu 1986). If, however, some do perform well, then it may be expected that others should do so. This then causes some to feel pressured to perform. To avoid this pressure, they try to limit the performance of those doing well. The argument makes sense, but I have found limited support for it based upon my data. Some support, to be sure, but less than I had expected.

Unlike Ms. Knowles, Ms. Love believes that racial discrimination plays a role in her life. She says that her upbringing "was hell" but did not elaborate, and she very much believes in discipline in raising her children. She states that she reads a book six days a week, unlike Ms. Knowles who does so once or twice a week, and she relies upon God, the church, and herself when she has a problem.

Raven, the sixth grader, most likes lunch and science in school, and least likes social studies, music, and curiously, the food at lunch. She believes that she is doing "very well" in school. Given her grades, her sense of her accomplishment may be a bit high, but not outrageously so. She believes that education is "kind of important" to her, but thinks that school is a way for parents to "get rid of their kids." It does not appear that she is particularly focused upon her education. Supporting her mother's contention, she says that another student did in fact try to stop her from doing well in school by distracting her from her schoolwork. She believes that this happened because some children are "misbehaved."

Raven indicates that she does no homework at all, instead doing her schoolwork at school. Given that we know that doing schoolwork at home, especially with the support and help of a parent (Sampson 2002), is important to the academic success of students, this causes some concern about her long-term academic success. She expects to complete college, and sees nothing standing in her way. She is particularly close to a specific sixth-grade teacher because that teacher helps her with her problems. Like her mother, she sees racial discrimination as a problem because "people should not judge." She says that she receives a lot of help with her schoolwork from her grandmother, some help from her mother, and a lot of help with her math from her dad. Her birth father lives in another state. However, she has indicated that she does no schoolwork at home, so it is not clear just how much help the family members can give to her. If she could be any other person in the world, that person would be Ashanti, because she has a "nice body, nice hair," and is rich.

During the first visit to Raven's home, the observer noted that Raven was open, friendly, and upbeat, her apartment was clean and neat (unlike Raven's bedroom), and at no time during the visit, which lasted several hours, did Raven do any schoolwork, nor did her mother ask about her school day. However, during the next visit, Raven was sitting on the couch in front of the television doing homework while watching music videos. While this suggests that she may not have been concentrating much on the homework (spelling), it also contradicts her answer to the question about the amount of time devoted to homework. Her brother, Andrew, who was also observed for this research, was asleep in his room. This was a weekday afternoon, a time when most good students are engaged in schoolwork.

Raven worked on the spelling for some thirty to forty minutes, and indicated that she was doing the work on this day so that she did not have work to do on the weekend. She did indicate that she generally does not bring work home from school because she completes the work at school, given that teachers give her time at the end of the day to complete the work. The students whom I studied in the same community, the same neighborhood, for the most part attending the same school, four years ago (Sampson 2002) who did well in school had largely the same routine: they came home from school, often after participation in extracurricular activities, settled into their homework, often with the help and support of a parent, and either ate dinner or performed household chores before returning to their homework.

This routine suggests discipline, responsibility, the ability to delay gratification, internal control, and perhaps high self-esteem (Clark 1983; Sampson 2002, 2003; Ford 1993; Comer 1993). Each of these characteristics is positively associated with academic achievement. Yet neither Raven nor Ashley Knowles, both of whom are above-average students, follows any part of this "routine." On the other hand, neither is an outstanding student. It may well be that both young ladies are sufficiently bright and motivated to do well without the "routine." Given that they are both in the sixth grade, it may be that the schoolwork is not yet difficult enough for them to need the routine. It is also possible that the school experience has become less rigorous for these young ladies. What we do know for certain is that they do not do much homework or household chores or engage in extracurricular activities that we could see, nor do they receive much direct support for their schoolwork from parents.

After completing her homework, Raven watched the television for the next hour, while telling the observer jokes and family stories. During the next visit, however, Raven was in fact doing household chores. This was the first time that any of the three students discussed thus far was observed doing chores. As I have indicated, the chores themselves are less important than the lessons they teach the student about responsibility and discipline, both of which are very important to academic success. After the chores, it was back to movie watching on the television. When Ms. Love arrived, she asked Raven and Andrew to take groceries from her car, and asked Raven to put them away. When Raven completed the task, she returned to watching the television, while Ms. Love prepared dinner, with Andrew peeling potatoes. Neither student did any schoolwork.

The next visit took place on a day when both Raven and her brother had a half-day of school due to parent-teacher conferences. Raven informed the observer that she had watched music videos since noon (the observer arrived at 4:30 p.m.). Ms. Love does not allow Raven or Andrew to go out and "hang around" when she is not at home. According to Raven, she becomes so bored when confined to the house that she just watches the television the entire time. Of course, she could read a book, but we never saw her do this. As she watched the videos, Raven told the observer about a sixth-grade friend who had become pregnant by a seventh-grade boy. Ms. Love told Raven not to spend time with the young lady because she was a "bad influence" on Raven.

The conversation then shifted to Raven's cell phone. The fact that a poor sixth grader had a cell phone was a bit surprising to the observer, but Raven assured her that almost all of the students at her middle school had cell phones. In fact, if they did not, they were "not normal," according to Raven. Two hours were spent watching music videos and discussing the pregnancy and an upcoming wedding. No time was devoted to chores or homework.

Raven watched the television for an hour and a half during the next visit, while Ms. Love remained in her bedroom and Andrew played video games. A bit later, Ms. Love emerged to go to a class, and Raven decided to do some schoolwork. Ms. Love said nothing to her about her work or about her school day. This was somewhat different from the next visit during which Raven cooked dinner for her mother, while Andrew played video games, as usual. Ms. Love explained to the observer that she wanted both of her children to become self-sufficient and to not be a burden to anyone else, to become independent.

Ms. Love went on to explain that several months ago Raven had discussed with her the taking of her own life, which led to a serious "fight" between the two. Ms. Love was not at all pleased with Raven's behavior at the time. Still, Raven managed to do above average in the classroom. Ms. Love's upbringing was, according to her, very strict, very rigid, with her having been beaten by her mother for not properly cleaning a dish pan and awakened during the night by her mother to wash and dry dishes, even though they had already been washed and dried earlier. She indicated that while she was quite strict with Raven, she was not nearly as strict with her as her own mother had been with her. She also indicated that she was just beginning to accept compliments positively, given that as a youngster she believed that her name was "bitch" or "hoe" or "dumb ass," and that these were the names most often used for her by the adults around her. Given this background, it is perhaps not surprising that we saw no real effort on the part of Ms. Love to raise the self-esteem of her two children, even though high self-esteem is important to academic success. After the chat with Ms. Love ended, Raven indicated that she was about to complete her household chores and go to bed.

When the observer arrived for the final visit, the children were at the local pharmacy picking up items for Ms. Love to eat. After they arrived home and shared a joke with Ms. Love, Raven showed everyone a book that she had gotten from school and about which she was quite excited. Ms. Love read a few pages to determine whether it was appropriate for Raven to read. The observer and Raven then went into another room to play a game while chatting about books, with Raven indicating that she loved to read. She did no homework, but did say that she intended to read that evening.

Like Bempechat (1998), Clark (1983), and Gutman and McLoyd (2000), I found in my earlier work (Sampson 2002) that homes in which the atmosphere was quiet, orderly, and structured, and in which the child being observed had high self-esteem, was disciplined, could delay gratification, was internally controlled, involved in extracurricular or household chores, and in which the parent inquired about schoolwork, imposed order, helped with homework, and imposed discipline produced high-achieving poor black students. In the case of the Love and the Knowles families, two students managed to show above-average school achievement though many of these characteristics are missing. We did observe Raven doing some household chores and a bit of schoolwork, though her mother never helped with that work, and we did see Ms. Love impose discipline. The home environment was not exactly the ideal environment, and Raven and her mother did not show many of the characteristics normally associated with high achievers. On the other hand, the poor black students observed for my earlier work who were considered high achievers had grades of A and B, and not the C and B grades that Raven and Ashley achieved. Actually, those grades would be average in my earlier work, but compared to the other students in this research, the grades are above average. In fact, they are above average by most accounts, though not high. So it may be that we do not see many of the characteristics of the homes or the students of high achievers because these two young ladies, while doing well, are not high achievers.

Raven's brother, Andrew, is average in the classroom. In the latest grading period he received one B, two Cs, and one D. In the first period, he received three Bs and a C grade. While one teacher indicated that he lacked self-control, two others suggested that he had a positive attitude. There are no serious indications of behavioral problems with Andrew. Ms. Love indicates that Andrew's education is "vital," "life or death" to her, because she does not want him to be "uneducated," as she was for some time. To encourage him, she "threatens to beat his brains out" and tries to explain just why his education is important. She says that she e-mails his teachers four times a week, but that she is "angry" when she visits his school. She feels this way because of the environment (children swearing) and because of the lack of communication between parents and teachers, which makes participation difficult.

Ms. Love believes that the absence of support at school and Andrew himself stand in the way of his educational success, but points out that no other child has tried to impede his success, unlike the case with Raven. She believes that his teachers only want a paycheck, as opposed to wanting to give all children a quality education, and believes that race plays a role in her life. She had a very difficult upbringing, including experiences that I elect not to mention here, but which are horrific. Ms. Love tries to make Andrew independent and safe, and tries to listen to him and pay attention to his wants. She says that discipline is big, and wants him to learn manners, etiquette, how to carry himself. She is "always on him about doing things the right way." She certainly sounds like a concerned, involved parent. The question is always whether the concern is translated into actions that properly prepare the student for the learning experience.

Andrew is a twelve-year-old seventh grader at the same middle school attended by his sister and most others from their neighborhood. He most likes the principal and least likes the teachers in his school. A dislike of teachers is probably not a good prerequisite for academic success. He believes that he is doing fair in school, suggesting that he knows where he stands. School is important to him because he wants to be a "robot engineer," and this requires an education. He ties education to the job market as opposed to his development, but this is not uncommon for younger students.

Andrew says that he devotes about an hour per day to his homework, but as will be shown, the observations suggest otherwise. When asked how far he expects to go in school, he answered the "middle of high school," indicating he wants to become an engineer but does not even expect to graduate from high school. Either Andrew has no real concept of the education–job link or has very low expectations. Neither is good for his academic success. He does not think much about race or racial discrimination because "it's boring," and says that he does not often get help with his schoolwork from his parents, another bad sign for his academic success. He does not know or care about being any other person in the world.

During the first visit to the Love household by the observer assigned to Andrew, Ms. Love noted that she was studying to become an assistant and that she had been illiterate until she was twenty-five years old. This would have made it impossible for her to read to her children when they were younger, and perhaps to understand their report cards and school reports once they entered school. Still, she has tried to involve herself in school activities only to become frustrated by the failure of the teachers to effectively communicate with her. While Andrew responded to the questionnaire in his bedroom, the television was on the entire time. When asked by Ms. Love to make sure that their rooms were neat because there was a guest in the home, both Raven and Andrew "obediently" went to straighten up their rooms. Andrew and Raven were described by this observer as "quiet" and "pleasant," but Ms. Love referred to Andrew as "meek" several times in his presence, probably not the best way to raise or support his self-esteem.

Andrew played video games, watched the television, and played with a remote-control car the entire time that the observer was in his home the next visit. His father, who is not his birth father, arrived from work and asked a few questions about the study, but he was not observed to play any role in the education or upbringing of the children at any time during our visits to see either Raven or Andrew. Andrew did no schoolwork at all during this visit, and instead devoted the entire time to the games and watching the television. This visit took place on a Sunday, however, and it may be that Andrew has a different routine on nonschool days.

The next visit took place on a Tuesday and Andrew did little other than watch the television that day as well. Neither parent was at home for the entire visit, so there was no one to ask about the school day; no one to make certain that the home environment was quiet, orderly, or structured; no one to impose discipline; no one to help with the homework; and no one to make certain that chores were done. Andrew watched the television during the entire time of the next visit as well. The only change to the pattern this time was that his father yelled at a young cousin who was visiting to "Shut the fuck up"—probably not the best thing to say to a four- or five-year-old or for Andrew to hear from an adult in his home.

At the time of the next visit, Ms. Love stayed in her bedroom the entire time until she left for work/school. She did not ask about school, help with schoolwork, supervise chores, or compliment the children. Andrew did, however, spend forty-five minutes on his homework, which consisted of reading three pages and four follow-up questions. However, the radio was on in his room the entire time. He asked the observer a question about the reading assignment because he had not had the opportunity to ask his mother even though she was in her bedroom, suggesting that he might sometimes talk to her about his homework. We saw no evidence of this during our visits with either Raven or Andrew, however.

When the schoolwork was completed, Andrew turned on the television and started to play video games, which is what he did during the next visit as well, though this time neither parent was at home. He interacted with his sister while they watched the television, but did little else. This pattern of almost no parental involvement with the children, no effort to talk about school or help with schoolwork, no effort to boost the self-esteem of the child, no effort to make certain that the home environment is quiet and orderly, no effort to make certain that the children are involved in activities that teach them to be responsible and to delay gratification is very different from that seen in the homes of high-achieving poor black students (Clark 1983; Sampson 2002).

Andrew and his sister are, however, not high achievers, but Raven is above average. It would seem that the home environment and achievement orientation are not exactly conducive to high achievement.

THE BAILEY/CHAMBERS FAMILY

Two different last names are used for this family because one of the sisters observed wanted to be known as Catrina Bailey and the other as Beyonce

Chambers. Catrina is a twelve-year-old seventh grader who, like her sister, attends the same middle school attended by all of the other poor black students discussed so far in this work—not surprising, given that they all live in the same neighborhood. For the fall grading period, Catrina received two Ds, two Cs, one A, and one B. I would classify her as an average student overall. Her teachers note no behavioral problems. Her mother, whom we shall term Ms. Bailey for both of the sisters, is forty years old and has lived in Evanston all of her life. She lives with her three children and another adult, and is herself unemployed, though she has worked in the health-care field. She is single and has completed two years at a community college.

Ms. Bailey indicates that Catrina's education is very important to her, a belief shared by almost all of the poor black and poor Latino parents observed. She wants her girls to do better than she has done, and she says that she tries to encourage Catrina to do well in school by helping her, asking about her homework, and attending parent-teacher conferences. She visits her school four or five times a year, and she feels "concerned" when she visits the school. She feels this way because she wants to know what is going on and isn't receiving an adequate response. She does not believe that anything stands in Catrina's way in terms of getting a good education. She believes that other children have tried to stop Catrina from doing well in school, though she offers no support for this belief. She does believe, however, that Catrina is "no problem" and is a "very good girl," and that her sister, Beyonce is "very bright" but "clowns around with a crowd that shows off."

Ms. Bailey does not believe that race or racial discrimination is a factor in her life. In discussing her upbringing she notes that it was very strict, that she went to Catholic schools and was separated from "bad kids," and that her mother was a single mother due to the death of Ms. Bailey's father. She raises Catrina to respect adults, to have an honest and open relationship with her, and to know that she is her friend. She reads a newspaper every day, loves books, and relies upon her brother-in-law "sometimes," and upon her sister and brother. She adds that she does not know whether she is doing the right things in terms of raising her daughters, but that she feels that she is. She tries her hardest.

As for Catrina, about school she most likes math (she is an A math student) and seeing her friends, and likes least all of the schoolwork both in school and at home, and points out that the work has increased since she has become a seventh grader. She believes that she is doing well in school, and that her education is "very important" to her. This is the case because, according to Catrina, one cannot get "anywhere without education." According to her, no other student has tried to stop her from doing well, contradicting her mother. She says that she spends an hour and a half a day on homework and that she does most of the work in class, so that she does not have to do it at home. If this is true, it suggests that not very much is going on in her classes if she has an hour and a half a day to do the work during class time.

She would like to go to law school and mentions Michigan State and Lincoln University, a historically black college attended by a cousin who tells her about the school. She sees no obstacles in her way. Catrina reads a newspaper twice a week (her mother does so every day, according to Ms. Bailey), and education and family are most important in her life. Catrina feels especially close to one of her summer school teachers because the teacher told her things that her former college basketball coach said to encourage her. Race or racial discrimination is not something about which she thinks, and she believes that race will not be an issue for her as long as she does her work. So, it appears that she does in fact believe that race is an issue, but that it is overcome by good and/or hard work.

According to Catrina, she receives "a lot" of help with her schoolwork from her mother, who is "a good writer," and she notes that her uncle is good at math. She apparently won an essay contest with her mother's help. She received Cs in both reading and language arts. If she could be any one person in the world, that person would be Maya Angelou, the renowned black poet, because she "expresses herself in poems." Catrina notes that she herself writes poems and believes that she will someday be famous. High hopes for a poor young black student, perhaps especially an average student, but great accomplishments begin with high hopes.

The observer met with Catrina at Family Focus for the first observation because Ms. Bailey was not going to be at home that evening. While Catrina and the observer went over a questionnaire, Catrina informed the observer that she plays on a basketball team that practices in the morning and requires her to awaken at 5:45 a.m. She also told the observer that she likes to go to school in order to spend time with her friends, and the observer noted that she appeared both friendly and to have a number of friends.

When the observer arrived on a Friday evening for the first observation at the Bailey home, Catrina was sitting at a desk doing homework, and her sister, Beyonce, was sitting on a sofa reading a book. Catrina was studying for a test required of all Illinois students, and her mother both examined her work and helped her with it. Her grandmother was present, as was her uncle a bit later. Ms. Bailey talked to Catrina about being overwhelmed by the test, and about how she at times felt overwhelmed by her new duties as a recent volunteer. There had been no school on this Friday, and Catrina was still studying and working on her worksheet, which was not due until the next Tuesday. Both she and her mother were proud of this, and Ms. Bailey let Catrina know that she was proud of her. This kind of praise is very important in building the self-esteem of a student, and high self-esteem in critical to academic success, as is the kind of discipline shown by Catrina in this instance, and the help with the schoolwork given by Ms. Bailey.

When finished with her worksheet, Catrina chatted with her sister and her mother, though Beyonce was on the telephone quite a bit. Ms. Bailey at one point told her to limit her conversation to five minutes and proceeded to time her talk until she hung up five minutes later, an example of the kind of discipline that often helps students to do well in school. Ms. Bailey then expressed concern to the observer about a student at Northwestern University in Evanston who had begun to serve as an intern at Family Focus and had, according to Ms. Bailey, shown a bit too much interest in Catrina. The student had called and asked to pick up Catrina to go to make cookies, and Ms. Bailey, while permitting this, was upset at the interest shown in her daughter by a young lady who had not bothered to introduce herself to Ms. Bailey. Ms. Bailey gave Catrina a time to return home, and as she left yelled to her, "No later than 7:30/8:00 for those cookies. I know it doesn't take that long for some cookies. I'm being nice." The next two observations took place at Family Focus and involved no schoolwork and little direct contact with Catrina or with Beyonce, who were involved in various group activities.

Beyonce Chambers is a ten-year-old sixth grader at the middle school attended by her sister. For the fall grading period she received four grades of C and one F, in reading. One of her teachers noted that she does not work independently and fails to make constructive use of her time. Her grades suggest that she is an average to slightly below-average student, and her mother suggested in comments to the observers that she is somewhat more difficult to deal with than her sister.

When asked what she most likes about school, Beyonce replied, "Allied arts, reading, writing, and art class," yet she received an F in reading. She least likes music, and believes that she is doing well in school. She believes that her education is very important because "You can't get very far without it." She wants to be a physician. According to her, no other student has tried to stop her from doing well in school. She says that she does a lot of her homework in school and at Family Focus, and does not have to do much at home. We did not see her do any schoolwork at Family Focus during the two times we observed her there. She would like to attend college and sees no obstacles in her way.

Beyonce believes that her education and family are the most important things in her life, and believes that her science teacher sometimes responds to the questions of white students while ignoring black students. She indicates that her mother helps her "a lot" with her homework and checks her math and writing assignments, and that her uncle helps her with math. However, this conflicts with her indication that she does little schoolwork at home. If she could be any one person in the world, she would be Beyonce Knowles, the singer and performer.

The observer assigned to Beyonce walked with her from Family Focus to her apartment for the first observation at her home, and was greeted by Beyonce's grandmother, who lives with the girls and their mother. Beyonce began to work on a school project that involved making a guest list, preparing a menu, and an introduction and conclusion for a birthday party for a celebrity. Catrina looked through a scrapbook about her "role model," Ashanti, the same black performer so admired by Raven Love. When Ms. Bailey arrived, she immediately told both girls to do their homework, and sat down with Beyonce to go over her project with her. This attention to the student's work and help from the parent is very important to academic success, but must be consistent.

The next time that the observer met with Beyonce, the meeting took place at Family Focus and revolved around an earlier incident involving Beyonce. It seems that she was involved in a fight with a young boy at Family Focus. Ms. Bailey was there to attempt to work things out,

though she was very angry with the teacher whose son had been involved in the fight. It seems that she believed that the teacher solely
blamed Beyonce for the fight. Almost in tears, Ms. Bailey apologized to
the observer that she had to see this side of Beyonce (her temper). The
observation ended when Ms. Bailey went to talk with a Family Focus
staff member about the altercation. Because several other scheduled
observations were cancelled, we were not able to observe this family as
often as we would have liked.

We did, however, learn that the mother pays some attention to the
schoolwork of her daughters, exerts some discipline, and expects some
responsibility from them. The home environment was not the most conducive to high academic achievement, and the students do not show the
self-esteem, ability to delay gratification, involvement in extracurricular
activities, or attention to schoolwork normally seen among the better
students. On the other hand, they were observed doing some schoolwork, did pay attention to the directions of their mother, and they are
average students. They are not poor black students doing nothing in
school and paying no attention to their academic lives. Although they do
not appear to be focused upon those academic lives, neither do they
completely ignore them.

THE AMJAD FAMILY

Sansara Amjad is a twelve-year-old Latina who lives with her mother, father, and five siblings, including her sixteen-year-old brother, Kuyo, who
was also observed. Sansara attends a middle school different from the
one attended by the other students observed thus far, and her grades are
average. She received two Cs, one B, one A, and one D for the first-term
grading period. The A grade was in an ESL (English as a Second Language) course. It was her father who answered the questions for the
questionnaire, a notable change from the pattern for the black families,
in which the father was either not present or was not visible during the
observations.

Mr. Amjad has lived in Evanston for sixteen years, grew up in Mexico,
and has lived in his current house for five years. He is a thirty-four-year-
old truck driver. His wife, Ms. Amjad, was born in Mexico but grew up

in Evanston, and completed the eighth grade. Mr. Amjad also completed the eighth grade, and thinks that Sansara's education is very important to him because his family has never had a member to go to college, and he would like to see her do so. He encourages her to do well in school by reminding her every day just how important education is, and says that he visits her school two or three times a week. When he does so, he feels comfortable and happy overall. This is the case because he is happy to see his daughter doing well in school, and is somewhat different from the feelings of several of the poor black parents interviewed thus far.

Mr. Amjad does not believe that other students try to stop Sansara from doing well in school, nor does he believe that race or discrimination plays a role in his life. His upbringing was difficult financially but happy, and he believes that discipline is important in raising Sansara, as is talking to her. He reads a newspaper every day, and reads a book at least ten minutes a day. His wife is his biggest source of support.

Sansara indicates that she most likes her math class when asked what she likes most about school, and least likes social studies. She believes that she is doing pretty good or fair in school, which seems to be an accurate judgment on her part. As is the case for just about all of the students observed, she indicates that education is very important to her, because it allows one to "get a good job." She does not think that any other student has tried to stop her from doing well, spends three hours per evening on her homework, and expects to go to college. She sees no obstacles in her way. For Sansara, her family is the most important thing in her life, and she feels close to a teacher at her school who is a family friend.

Sansara does not think about race, and receives "a lot" of help from her parents with her schoolwork, as much as five times a day, though even this is not enough help in her opinion. She would change nothing about her life if she could make any changes, and would be her mother if she could be any other person in the world. This is a very different answer from those given by the young poor black females, who tend to want to be glamorous black performers, and might say something about the value of the family to this young Latina. Indeed, in my earlier work with poor Latino families (Sampson 2003), it was clear that the family was a critical institution for them, more so than appeared to be the case for poor blacks.

The observer for the Amjad family noted that their living quarters were very small and cramped. There were two bedrooms for the eight family members in their basement apartment, but she also noted, "the family was so loving." During the first visit, the two older boys were at work, and two younger brothers and the father were at home. A five-year-old brother was practicing his English, and Mr. Amjad constantly hugged his children, the kind of show of affection that helps with the children's self-esteem. As Sansara talked with the observer, she told her that she never planned to move away from her family because they meant so much to her. During the visit, Sansara did no schoolwork but did go outside to play with her brothers and cousins who live upstairs.

During the second visit, the observer was again offered something to drink by Sansara, and noted that "she seemed like a second mother to her brothers," an interesting observation about a twelve-year-old. However, in an earlier work (Sampson 2003), it was also noted that many of the young Latinas seemed to play the same role, and appeared to be raised to be wives and mothers, as opposed to successful scholars. This bears watching. As they watched the television, the observer and Sansara talked about a variety of things, with Sansara asking most of the questions and talking about the birthday party for her younger brother. They then played a video game for an hour and a half until Mr. Amjad arrived home, hugged and kissed all of the children, and began to prepare food for the children. Sansara then began to clean the house and to help her father prepare the food. So she did household chores but no homework.

Indeed, the observer noted after her next visit, "I can tell that education is important to their family, but whenever I am over at their home I never see Sansara studying." When asked about homework, Sansara replied that she had Spanish homework. I should note that to this point all discussion in the house was in English, though it is mainly Spanish that is spoken in the home. Sansara rushed through her homework assignment and told the observer that she was finished. The observer noted, "She doesn't seem very interested in school, she seems like she's more into having a fun social life." She then told the observer that her parents do not allow either her or her fifteen-year-old sister to date, and that they are very strict.

Sansara told the observer that she was not doing very well in school in Spanish, and this despite the fact that Spanish is often spoken in the home.

The rest of the visit was spent watching a movie and playing outside—again, very little attention to school, and no help from a parent.

Indeed, during the next observation, the entire family was present and none of the children did any schoolwork or opened a book. Neither parent read to a child or talked to a child about school. The observer described the family as "welcoming and sweet," "nice and warm," and "close and caring," but no schoolwork was done. The observer noted that she never saw Sansara studying. Ms. Amjad cooked dinner, cleaned the rooms, and discussed the family's lack of money. Looking at the gas and cell-phone bills, she said, "This is why poor people stay poor." The observer noted that "all" of the children have cell phones, and wondered why a family of eight living in a two-bedroom apartment has so many cell phones. It is really not up to us to make judgments about how families should spend their money, but this is interesting.

During the visit, Ms. Amjad became upset with her children because they failed to clean their rooms. She noted that she works full time, while the children have nothing to do and should clean the rooms. In reality, the parents should teach the children that this is their responsibility. If they do not learn to accept and carry out responsibility at home, it is unlikely that they will do so in school. When she grumbled about the lack of responsibility on the part of the children, one son replied, "Mom, this is your job." His mother ignored the comment and continued to clean.

Sansara was working on her English assignment when the observer next visited. The observer noted that she had trouble spelling rather simple words such as "geese," "crackers," and "hear," words that should pose no problem for a seventh grader. She asked the observer to help her, but neither of her parents was seen helping her at any time during our observations, despite what she said during the interview. While working on the assignment, Sansara constantly complained that she was tired and just wanted to finish the work.

After completing the English work with the help of the observer, Sansara moved on to history, but when her cousins arrived she "forgot" about the work and began to play with them. She did this for an hour, throwing darts, speaking funny phrases, and just "goofing off." After playing she began to sweep the family room. Ms. Amjad arrived soon after, along with a brother and sister. It was report card day and one child had received three grades of F, and "her parents didn't even care," according to the observer. In fact, "they made a joke of it."

Despite the professed value for education, little evidence of its importance was seen in what the family members did during our five visits. Little schoolwork was done; the parents did not help with the work; the children showed little responsibility in the home; there was no evidence of involvement in extracurricular activities; the parents imposed no order; and the home environment, while loving and relaxed, lack the order, structure, and quiet seen in homes in which children tend to do well in school.

Kuyo, a sixteen-year-old tenth grader at the local high school, lives in the same environment. He received grades of F in all five of the subject-area courses he took, and his teachers noted that he was often absent from class. His father noted that he sometimes has a bad attitude, that he sometimes does not care what others think.

Kuyo, for his part, about his school most likes the girls and one teacher, and least likes the fact that he must wake up to go to school. He knows that he is not doing so well in school, and thinks that his education is "kind of important," because although he does not like school, without it he cannot get a job. He believes that his "enemies" try to prevent him from doing well in school by trying to fight with him so that he will be suspended and cannot learn that which he should learn—an interesting justification for failure. They do this, according to Kuyo, because "they are haters."

Kuyo receives no homework because he is in alternative school, according to him, and he therefore devoted no time to schoolwork. Yet he says that he receives "a lot" of help with the work from his parents. He would like to receive a master's degree, and in fact expects to do so. This is an enormous stretch for a student receiving all Fs!

Kuyo says that he reads a newspaper every day, and that his family is the most important thing in his life, the same as his sister. He does not think about race because he does not "care what people say about my race."

During the first visit to the Amjad home to meet with Kuyo, the observer discovered that he was not at home, so he spent his time there interviewing Mr. Amjad and looking around the house. He noted that Mr. Amjad needed some help with his English from his daughter, and that the apartment is very small. When the observer next visited the home,

Kuyo arrived soon after the observer, showed him his room, which was described as "as a half-way converted storage closet" by the observer. Kuyo pointed to a small, worn carpet and tells the observer that he "throws parties" in the area in which the rug is located.

As Kuyo deals with his questionnaire, Ms. Amjad cooks dinner and tells the observer that she has had children since she was fourteen years old. Kuyo explains that he has no homework because at his alternative high school homework is not given, and explains that the alternative school is a "school for the bad kids." He tells the observer that he goes to the gym daily, that he parties only with girls because boys just fight, flash gang signs, and posture when they are at parties or drinking. He indicates that he is not interested in any of this, but is only interested in girls. When asked his plans for life after high school, he replies that he isn't certain, but that he might join the Armed Forces or go to college and then get a "cushy" job. During the observation, the younger siblings twice ask Kuyo to let them play video games, which are located in his room. He replies without question the first time, but expresses his annoyance the second time.

When Kuyo arrived for the third observation, the observer asked him just what he did when he got home from school, and Kuyo answered, "just chill mostly," and proceeded to play a video game. A short time later, Mr. Amjad came in with two armloads of laundry, said hello, and left to finish the laundry. Two interesting points here. First, this is really the first time that we have observed a father involved in any household activities, and second, Kuyo has not been involved in any of the household chores or activities other than eating and playing games. For the most part, raising the children and preparing them for school, to the extent that the latter is done, appears thus far to be the mother's role, as does doing the various household chores.

When Ms. Amjad arrived, the children clamored for dinner, and as she began to prepare the meal she lamented the fact that she works all day and gets no time to rest as her children want dinner immediately. Kuyo and his sister discussed the responsibility for Ms. Amjad's high cell-phone bill, then he went to install speakers in his mother's van and returned to his room to play another video game.

The next time that the observer visited, Kuyo was feeling ill—the effects, Kuyo surmises, of staying up late and "partying" the last few days.

He and the observer played a video game for an hour and a half while his younger brothers watched. They then went into the living room to sit with the parents and siblings. Mr. Amjad had apparently not done well on an exam and was feeling badly about this, and Kuyo talked to his mother about problems with his girlfriend. He found his girlfriend to be too controlling because she had asked him not to drink too much, and she was upset with him for asking her not to go out with her friends. A few minutes later, the family dog returned to the house, was let in by Kuyo, and promptly urinated on the floor. Kuyo refused to clean up after the dog, forcing his sister to do the task even though she was preparing dinner while Ms. Amjad dealt with a headache. Kuyo then decided to go to bed.

The final visit saw no real changes: Kuyo and the family ate dinner while talking in Spanish, Kuyo watched the television (the show was in Spanish), and then talked by phone with his girlfriend. No homework was done by any of the children, nor did they do any housework. The parents, of course, did not help with any schoolwork. No newspapers or books were read by anyone; there was no discussion of school at all; there was almost constant noise from the television; no children were seen to be involved in any extracurricular activities; there was no structure to the home environment; there was no visible effort on the part of the parents to raise Kuyo's self-esteem; and there was very little supervision of the children's activities. Indeed, Kuyo did what he wanted, including brag about his drinking (even though he is only sixteen years old). So, although Mr. Amjad expresses his interest in and concern for the education of his children, there is virtually no attempt to properly prepare them for school.

THE MARTINEZ FAMILY

Esmeralda Martinez is a fifteen-year-old girl who is currently being taught at home in Evanston. She began the academic year in a high school in Chicago, and has been schooled at home for about three weeks. Her grades for the fall term from that high school included three Cs, one B, and one D, though she did receive an A and a B in physical education and band respectively. This makes her an average student.

She lives with her thirty-six-year-old mother, her father, and two siblings in Evanston, and has lived in her current house for seven months. Mr. Martinez works in a meat packing facility, grew up in Mexico, and completed the second grade in school. His wife completed the American equivalent of the first two years of high school in Mexico. She says that Esmeralda's education is important to her because it is important for her future, it will benefit her. She tries to encourage Esmeralda to do well in school by telling her to study, to go to school, and notes that Esmeralda has a problem with school. When Esmeralda was in school, her mother says that she visited the school to pick up the report cards and to find out how she was doing. When she visited, according to Ms. Martinez, how she felt depended upon the questions that she asked. She indicated that she was not afraid to ask questions and that she always requested a translator.

Ms. Martinez believes all of the teachers are (were) good, and notes that nothing really stands in the way of Esmeralda doing well in school. She says, however, that other students have tried to tell Esmeralda to misbehave, to skip school, to run away from home. This is not the kind of pressure from students about which Fordham and Ogbu (1986) or myself (Sampson 2002) have written. This appears to go beyond peer pressure toward negative achievement. This is pressure toward a negative life experience.

Ms. Martinez does not believe that discrimination plays a role in her life, describes her upbringing as quiet, and notes that while she had few friends, she did like to party. She believes that it is important to control and maintain discipline with her children to keep them in line. She does not read a newspaper and only reads a book when she reads to her youngest son.

As I indicated, Esmeralda had been schooled at home for three weeks prior to the start of our observations, and planned to return to her Chicago-based high school at the beginning of the next academic year. She indicated that she likes school and her friends, but that she "hung out with the wrong crowd." She did not like the homework or the teachers telling her what to do or restricting her freedom. She believes that she did well in school, and that school was very important to her because it affects her future and her effort to become someone. She does not agree with her mother that other students tried to prevent her from doing well in school, and says that she spends one to two hours on her homework during the week and a half an hour a day on the weekends. She would like to go to a university and sees no obstacles in her way. Esmeralda does not read a newspaper and believes that her family is the most important thing in her life.

Neither race nor discrimination are things about which she thinks, but she adds that she knows people who degrade Mexicans and who do not believe that they can do well. She does not get much help with her schoolwork because "everything is in English," which they do not read. If she could change anything about her life, it would be to spend more time with her family.

When the observer arrived for the first visit with the Martinez family, Esmeralda and her mother were not at home but arrived shortly after. Esmeralda went to her room to do her homework. She was interrupted often by her two-year-old brother, who wanted to play. She informed the observer that she spends most days and nights with her godmother, and spends Tuesday and Thursday at the family home because of "the problems." The homeschooling is done at the godmother's home; while at her family home, she locks herself in her room and listens to music.

When her eleven-year-old brother came to the room to ask to use her computer because his did not work, she yelled at him to leave her room. After Mr. Martinez asked her to allow Ricardo to use the computer, she logged on for him, and left to watch television in her parents' room while the two-year-old played on the bed. The next visit began at Family Focus, and the observer offered to pick Esmeralda up and bring her home. Ms. Martinez agreed, but told the observer to make certain that Esmeralda accompanied her home. She seemed worried that Esmeralda would try to go somewhere else.

At the house, Esmeralda explained that she was being schooled at home because she got into trouble often at school. She missed classes often and ran away from home as well. Administrators at the school recommended that the family contact Family Focus to provide counseling for Esmeralda. The observer described the home as a small two-bedroom home. The parents and the two-year-old sleep in one bedroom (with the child), and Esmeralda and her twelve-year-old brother sleep in the other room, with him sleeping on a folding bed. Ms. Martinez told the observer about the problems Esmeralda had in school and asked for advice from the observer.

During the next observation, Esmeralda spent some time preparing a paper on the computer while her two brothers put a puzzle together on the floor. Esmeralda commented that the assignment was "boring"; when the work was complete, she and the observer went to her room and discussed school and boys. She said that she is not allowed to talk with boys on the telephone, and that includes the boy she considers to be her boyfriend. This appears to suggest that her parents believe that she has had involvement with boys whom they consider unacceptable. As the two young ladies talked, the two-year-old went in and out of the room, bothering them and interrupting the conversation. He did this for some time, though periodically his father or mother would call him into the living room. They did try to exert a bit of discipline.

Esmeralda explained that her mother and brother were probably going to visit Mexico during the school spring break, but she might not go along because she has a great deal of work to make up, basically starting her freshman year over since the start of her homeschooling. She does not like going to Mexico anyway because, according to her, the men are "perverts" who try to approach her and constantly call her "Mamacita," which she does not like. During the next visit, Esmeralda explained that her homeschooling was being done through a program, which at first used CDs and then switched to the use of textbooks as teaching tools. The credits that she will receive for the homeschooling can, according to her, be transferred to her high school when she returns in the fall, assuming that her parents allow her to return.

During each of the last two visits, Mr. Martinez watched the television while Ms. Martinez prepared dinner. Neither Esmeralda nor her brother did any household chores, no one helped Esmeralda with the very small amount of schoolwork that she did, and there was always noise from the television and from the two-year-old playing. At one point, the two-year-old played with a toy gun until his father "yelled" at him to stop, explaining that he should not play with a gun. Again, he tried to exert some discipline and had something to say about the behavior of at least the little boy.

Esmeralda was again using the computer to prepare a book report, but she stopped before completing the report and went to her room. Ricardo, the eleven-year-old, entered the room and asked the observer whether her younger brother, who played on the same soccer team, remembered him. Apparently, Ricardo is involved in some after-school activity. He had received his report card that day, and after showing it to his parents, Ms. Martinez came into the room to ask the observer to explain the grades to her, that is, to tell her whether they were good or bad grades. She admonished him for getting upset after she told him to do his homework rather than watching the television. This suggests that Ricardo might not pay the necessary attention to either his parent or his schoolwork.

The inability of the parents to read English is a problem. In this case, they could not even read or understand the child's report card, making it almost impossible for them to monitor his progress. When Ricardo asked his mother to sign the report card, she indicated that she wanted his father to take a look at it first. Again, the father appears to play a significant role in the raising of the children, at least the boys, and in the household. Remember that Mr. Amjad was the one to answer the questions for the questionnaires. We have not seen this level of involvement on the part of the black men in the homes. It is true, however, that the black women observed so far, for the most part, have been raising their children on their own, while the Latino families have had both parents present.

Esmeralda talked to the observer about how she had just gotten her ears pierced with a second hole, a party to which she was going soon, and a shopping trip to a suburban shopping mall with her cousin who was looking for dress clothes, but ended up buying "ghetto clothes" instead. During this time, she sat on her bed and listened to music while her youngest brother came in and out of her room looking for a book.

During the final visit, Ms. Martinez talked with the observer about how both Ricardo and Esmeralda needed to do better in school. This discussion took place while the television was on, and after Ms. Martinez got off of the telephone with her family in Mexico. She noted that she and her husband supply everything the children need and did not seem to understand why they could not perform better. She expressed concern for Esmeralda's return to high school, which was necessary because the godmother who apparently handled the homeschooling had just had a baby and could not continue to deal with the homeschool work. There will therefore be no one at home to "school her," and they do not have the money to pay a teacher full time. They will have no choice but to send her to a public school. She tells the observer, "[Esmeralda] does not want to go to the high school in Evanston. She wants to go back to her old high school, but I am afraid she might go back to what she did before. It would have been a relief if she would have run away with her boyfriend because then I would not have to worry."

This is a strange and troubling statement, to say the least. Clearly, Ms. Martinez is concerned about her daughter's education, but seems to have no idea at all about just what she needs to do to help her daughter to do well, and sounds so frustrated that she might prefer to see her gone rather than for the parents to have to continue to deal with her. Ms. Martinez told the observer that the children never have to wash the dishes, wash clothes, or help to prepare their meals. According to her, "They don't do anything." On the weekends they are taken out to eat. In her view, since they do nothing around the house, and are given "everything," they should do better in school. Apparently, they are not given that which they need at home to properly prepare them for the educational experience.

We did not see the orderly, structured home environment, or the efforts to teach delayed gratification or responsibility. We did not see the involvement of the parents with schoolwork. In fact, we saw very little schoolwork done by Esmeralda, and not once did either parent even ask about school. Esmeralda seems to go her own way, with very little control from her parents or on her own part.

Ms. Martinez, clearly frustrated, says that she is going to take everything away from the school-aged children if they do not do better in school. However, she believes that it is wrong to give them nothing, so she is uncertain just what to do. Mr. Martinez cannot read or write in either Spanish or English, and is not comfortable asking Esmeralda to translate almost everything for him. I observed much the same thing in my earlier work (Sampson 2003) with poor Latino families. Often, a parent cannot read English and a child is required to translate. This places a great burden upon the child to think and act like an adult well before he or she is ready. This is worse because Mr. Martinez cannot read at all, and because Esmeralda reads very little Spanish. Thus, basic things become huge projects for them. Mr. Martinez arrived soon with Esmeralda and a new personal computer, but they asked the observer to show them how to install everything.

Ricardo is an eleven-year-old sixth grader at one of the middle schools in Evanston, not the one attended by most of the students observed, though his family lives in the same neighborhood as those discussed thus far. For the fall grading period, he received three Cs and one B, and for the latest grading period he received three Cs and one A. He appears to be an average student. His teacher for three of the classes noted that he lacked self-control. Ricardo, when asked what he least likes about his school, replied that students "always talk trash." He thinks that he is doing pretty good in school, and that school is very important to him because his father tells him to stay in school. This does not suggest much thought on his part about his education and the role that it plays in his life. He is, however, only eleven years old.

Ricardo says that he spends thirty minutes a day during the week on schoolwork, and no time on the weekends. His educational goal is to complete high school and he likes the Army. I would have to say that his educational aspirations are rather modest. Remember, however, that his parents did not go very far in school. On the other hand, higher-achieving students tend to have high educational goals no matter the educational level of their parents, who, it would seem, have a large part of the responsibility for ensuring these high goals. He sees no obstacles in the way of his completion of high school. Ricardo's family is the most important thing in his life, he reads the newspaper once a week, and feels especially close to his sixth-grade teacher, whom he says treats him like a son.

He gets "a lot of help" from his parents with his schoolwork, and believes that this help is sufficient. Asked what one thing about his life he would change, Ricardo replied that he would get his dad a better job. If he could be one person in the world, it would be Dr. Martin Luther King because he would like to fight for his rights, or basketball player Scottie Pippin, so that he could play basketball.

The observer noted that during his first visit to the family home Ricardo mentioned that his parents were "always" checking with him to see that he had completed his homework, and that his family "only cared about finishing high school" and he therefore never really thought about going to college. This suggests the role that a parent may play in helping to set the child's educational goals and thereby affecting his academic performance. If Ricardo only wants to complete high school, why would he need to worry about doing very well in school? Decent grades will get him through high school, and even those are not required to get him into high school.

After completing the questionnaire, Ricardo and the observer went to Esmeralda's room. While the questionnaire was being completed, Ricardo's parents and younger brother watched the television. In fact, for the remainder of the time that the observer was in the home for this visit, Ricardo also watched the television, a Latin American baseball game. The observer noted that Ricardo and his father appear to have a "strong connection" when it comes to sports. When the observer arrived for the next visit, Mr. Martinez and his youngest son were again watching the television, this time a soccer match. The observer noted that while Mr. Martinez said little, paying a great deal of attention to the match, he did seem to be attentive to his son when he asked his father for a snack.

When Ricardo arrived with his mother and sister, he informed the observer in response to a question that he had completed his homework at Family Focus. While this may have been the case, it is also true that at Family Focus the students meet in groups, and often the group sessions are rather noisy with some students working and others talking and playing. Furthermore, this context does not allow a parent to ask about the schoolwork or to help the student with the work. The parent then learns nothing about the work or the student's connection to the work, and cannot send the message about just how important the work is by helping with it. Of course, this is very difficult if the work is in English and the parent speaks no English, which is the case here. But the effort on the part of the parent is important.

Ricardo spent the evening at the dinner table asking questions of the observer, watching the soccer match, and browsing through his mother's magazine. During the next visit, Mr. Martinez again watched a soccer match on the television while Ricardo played a computer game, after telling the observer that he had already completed his homework, and not responding to a question about what specifically he had done. The entire time was devoted to watching the television and playing computer games. In fact, Ricardo went into his parent's room the next visit to play a video game on the television in that room after telling the observer and his father that he had completed his homework after his father asked about the work. When pressed on this by the observer, Ricardo replied, "I did most of it, but not all of it," and the observer wrote that he realized that Ricardo probably does most of his work at Family

Focus but not all of it. Again, the atmosphere at the agency can be such that it is not very conducive to the completion of homework. Ricardo spent the evening playing video games and at no time did either parent check on him or talk with him about school, nor did he do any housework or read anything.

Ricardo played video games during the entire time that the observer was there next while his mother and brother watched the television. His father and sister were not at home. During the final observation, the entire family was in the living room watching a music video on the television. Ricardo then went to play computer games. His father did ask him whether he had completed his homework, and he replied, "Sí, papi," though his smile to the observer suggested to him that he had not really done the work. The pattern played out again: Ricardo played computer games while his family watched the television.

Although Mr. Martinez expressed a little interest in Ricardo's schoolwork, he did not really ever check to see that it was done. Neither parent asked about school, and the home was never quiet. Ricardo was not observed engaging in any extracurricular activities, though he appears to be on a soccer team. He does no household chores and was not seen doing any homework. His discipline can be questioned, given the amount of time he devotes to watching the television and playing games, and we saw little indication of high educational aspirations. His parents exerted no parental control and imposed little order. Ricardo seems to do that which he wants, and that is to play games. His educational aspirations are not high either. This is not a recipe for academic success, though Ricardo does manage to be an average student.

SUMMARY

"The interpersonal communication patterns in these homes tended to be marked by frequent parent-child dialogue, strong parental encouragement in academic pursuits, clear and consistent limits set for the young, warm and nurturing interactions, and consistent monitoring of how they used their time" (Clark 1983, 111). Clark wrote this about high achievers, and it does not really describe the family lives of the ten students observed for this chapter, though some of the elements were observed on occasion, but never consistently. The families show little evidence of high-achievement orientation or of the kind of discipline and rigidity on the part of parents found in the high- and even the average-achieving students observed in my earlier work (Sampson 2002).

For the most part, the black and Latino students observed for this chapter do much of what they want at home, and they rarely want to do homework or housework. Their parents rarely make certain that either are done, nor do the parents seem to go out of their way to compliment the students in order to raise their self-esteem. There was little involvement in the extracurricular activities that help to develop discipline, a sense of responsibility, and higher self-esteem, all required for high educational achievement.

In the case of both of the Latino families, the father is present in the home and was occasionally involved in dealing with the children and the home. That was not the case for the three poor black families, where the father was either not present or, in the one family in which he was present, was not seen playing much role in the preparation of the children for school or the running of the household. Having both parents present, in theory, allows a parent to devote more time and energy to the process of school preparation. However, we saw little evidence of this in either the one poor black home in which the father was present or the two poor Latino homes.

In the Martinez home, however, the parents speak only Spanish and the father does not read either English or Spanish. This makes it virtually impossible for them to help with homework that is done in English and may well lead to alienation from schools in which only English in spoken by most teachers. Both Esmeralda and Ricardo Martinez seem to do pretty much as they please with their lives, as does Kuyo Amjad, who as a high school sophomore, already drinks a fair amount of alcohol, apparently with the knowledge of his parents, and never studies. It appears that the Latino parents want the best for their children but have no idea just what to do about this. The homes seem to be warm and loving, but are not particularly conducive to high achievement. The students believe that education and family are very important to them, but do little to demonstrate the importance of education to them, and their parents, as I have indicated, do almost nothing about this.

Although Raven and Andrew Love do fairly well in school, their family life is not really a model for high achievement. Neither of them was observed doing housework on any consistent basis. Indeed, the observer was surprised to see Raven preparing dinner one evening. Neither did much homework (Andrew did almost none), and the television was on when Raven did her work. Sansara Amjad does fairly well in school as well, though her household is not at all conducive to high achievement, given the noise, the lack of order, and the lack of attention to discipline and responsibility.

In summary, these are not high-achieving students, and the home life, many of the student characteristics, and several of the characteristics of the parents seem to mitigate against high achievement. Still, several students manage to do fairly well, and there are some indications on occasion of the right things being in place in some of the homes.

4

SCHOOL PREPARATION AND
THE ABOVE-AVERAGE STUDENT

Only one student is included in this section even though three above-average students were observed. The other two students, Ashley Knowles and Raven Love, were included in the chapter on the five families in which more than one student was observed. Although they, perhaps, should have been included in this chapter, such a division would have made the comparisons with their siblings, who were also observed, a bit more difficult.

ANGELA KING

Angela King is an eleven-year-old fifth grader at the same elementary school attended by several other students in this study, but which is not located in the area near the neighborhood in which virtually all of the participating families live. For the latest grading period, Angela was at grade level in eight of twelve reading and writing categories, and at grade level with some intervention in four of the twelve categories. She was above grade level in two of three listening and speaking categories, and at grade level in the third. She was at grade level in eight of ten math categories, and at grade level with some intervention in the other two categories. She was at grade level in five of six science categories and above in the other. She was at grade level in all three social studies categories, and needed intervention to reach grade level in two special social studies categories. Angela is the only elementary grade student observed who was above grade level in any category, and although she needed some intervention to achieve grade level in several categories, I have rated her as an above-average student, especially when compared to the others in the study.

Her mother is a fifty-year-old mother of three who is divorced, has lived in Evanston for thirty-five years, and has been in her current house for five months. Ms. King works full time "doing taxes," but is considered disabled. She believes that Angela's education is very important because one's entire life depends upon education. She gives Angela both "spoken and unspoken encouragement" to do well in school, and said that she gives her "rewards and praise," which suggests that she has some idea of the importance of Angela's self-esteem for her educational success. This is something not seen or heard much among the seventeen families observed for this study, but seen and heard often among the six poor black families with high-achieving students studied four years ago (Sampson 2002). Students who lack high self-esteem will often struggle in school because they will have trouble accepting the criticism that often comes with not doing very well on an assignment or a test in school, or from not being prepared or paying attention. All students face some criticism; the issue is whether they are prepared to deal with it. High self-esteem helps prepare them to handle it better.

Ms. King says that she visits Angela's school eighteen or twenty times a year, and feels "happy and confident" when she does so. So, unlike some of the parents observed, there is no indication that she is intimidated by the school environment, as is the case for many poor nonwhite parents. Ms. King indicates that she visits Angela's school because she likes to stay involved "in a lot of school functions." Of course, the involvement of parents in school activities is a good predictor of academic achievement. However, it is not that the involvement itself translates into higher performance. Parents who are involved are more likely than others to do the things at home necessary to properly prepare their children for the educational experience. If Ms. King is as involved as she indicates she likes to be, then we might expect that she does many of the things at home that would, all other things being equal, lead to higher performance for Angela. I do not see this level of performance, however.

Ms. King does not believe that anything stands in her daughter's way in terms of her receiving a good education, and she does not believe that any other student has tried to limit her success. She does, however, think that an "older teacher" tried to get in Angela's way by holding her back a grade. I suspect that Angela's performance had more to do with her being held back than did any negative feelings for Angela on the part of an elementary school teacher. Ms. King does not believe that race or discrimination plays a role in her life.

In raising Angela, Ms. King says that she tries to explain to her right from wrong, and what is most important. She also teaches her that God is most important. She relies upon God when she has a problem, reads a newspaper daily, and a book once or twice a week.

When asked what she most liked about her school, Angela replied, "the students." She least likes the fact that the school is "not so clean," and thinks that she is doing well in school. Education is very important to Angela, though she did not tell us why this is the case. She does not believe that any other student has tried to prevent her from doing well in school, and she says that she devotes thirty minutes a day to her homework and another hour to reading. She would like to go "as far as possible" in school, and expects to go "until the end." These are not really specific educational goals, especially when compared to the goals of the other students interviewed, including students of her age.

Angela never reads a newspaper and, like most of the other young people interviewed, Angela thinks that her family is the most important thing in her life. Unlike most of the others, however, she also thinks that school is most important. She pays little attention to race or discrimination, and says that she receives help with her schoolwork from her mother "whenever I need it." If she could change one thing about her family life, it would be for all of her family to live together; if she could be any one person, that person would be Michael Jordan, the retired basketball player, "because he is the best in basketball." She went on to add that God is very close to her and is always there when she needs God. Clearly, both Angela and her mother have lives heavily influenced by religion.

When the observer first met with Angela at her home, Angela was sitting on a sofa watching a television show, though she had open books and papers next to her, suggesting that she had been involved with schoolwork as well as watching the television. When Ms. King emerged from her room, she talked with the observer about Angela's basketball team and an upcoming championship game, with both Angela and her mother showing excitement about the team's success.

Angela then returned to her homework while her mother returned to her bedroom. After forty-five minutes, Angela was finished with her homework. She then spent the rest of the evening watching the television. Ms. King came out of her room and explained to the observer that Angela on occasion goes to the local library to work on a school project because they do not have the "right equipment" for all of her projects. She appears to be a mother who is concerned with her daughter's schoolwork, but she said nothing to Angela about that work during the visit, nor did she offer to help with the homework.

Angela was not at home at the arranged time for the next visit, and the observer spent an hour and a half talking with her older sister and a cousin from out of town while waiting for her. They eventually walked to Family Focus to determine whether she was there. When they found that Angela was not at Family Focus either, the older sister called Ms. King, who was angry that she was not there and not at home. They returned to the King home, watched the television, and waited for Angela. The sister indicated that she would begin her homework after eating, but said that there was nothing to eat in the house. She talked about spending the five dollars she had on a meal from McDonald's.

Finally, Angela arrived and told everyone that she had been at the YMCA doing her homework with a friend. Her sister indicated that she was upset that Angela had failed to inform anyone of her location, and Angela pulled out her homework and began "doing some worksheets" while sitting in front of the television. She then went into the dining room to ask her brother for help with a math worksheet. When he could not really help her, they asked the observer for help. Angela then explained to the observer that while at the YMCA she, her friend, and the friend's mentor had actually worked on fliers to announce the fifth-grade talent show because she and some friends were responsible for the organization.

Angela is involved in basketball and in organizing the talent show. These activities help to build self-esteem, and to teach responsibility and discipline. It is not clear what Ms. King does to support this involvement. Angela did tell the observer that her older sister often helps her with her homework, and the sister helped a bit while the observer was there, but she "still seemed distant and more interested in her friends, the phone, and the television" than in helping Angela. Angela devoted half an hour to her homework and then watched the television, which was on the entire time that she worked on her homework.

The observer noted that there were large boxes and material stacked in the living room and hallway, and that it appeared that "much remained to be unpacked." Ms. King was not at the home for the visit, and none of the older children had begun any homework by 8:30 p.m., nor had they eaten dinner or done anything around the house. They watched the television and talked.

When the observer next visited the King home, Angela was again working on her homework on the sofa while watching the television. After about twenty minutes, she put the homework aside and focused on the television. Angela explained that her teacher was preparing them for an upcoming mass testing the next week, and that some of the math was "seventh-grade math," so she did not feel too badly that she did not understand all of the work, which according to the observer, she did not.

Her older sister arrived a bit later and was excited to tell Angela that she had in fact not been expelled from the track team, as had been understood a few days earlier. Rather, she had been suspended. She had thought that she was expelled for being in a fight, but was suspended for a different, and relatively minor, infraction. She said that she had learned a "life lesson" and would not do anything silly again that might result in her leaving the team. She seemed to be a fairly responsible young lady, capable of disciplining herself, but also open to discipline. She is teachable.

The sisters and the observer watched the television for the next hour while discussing various recording artists. They discussed the dental procedure that Angela had that morning, and they talked about college, with the older sister telling them that she had applied to a college in Louisiana because of the quality of their pre-med program. So, college is not just a distant idea to these young women, but a reality, suggesting fairly high educational aspirations. After this discussion, Angela returned to her homework, with her sister helping "intermittently."

When her sister went to her bedroom to talk on the phone, Angela used another phone to eavesdrop on the call, giggling occasionally. She then used a different phone to call a friend's cell phone and hang up time after time, laughing each time. She then returned to television watching and talking to the observer about playing professional basketball someday.

Despite what Angela and her mother said about helping with her homework, Ms. King never did that while the observer was in the home. Indeed, Ms. King was not there much herself. It is the case, however, that she has been very ill and when not in the home was either at the office of her physician or at the hospital. She was not there to ask about Angela's day, her school experience, to help with or monitor the homework, or to compliment her on anything that she did that day. Her older sister and brother were there for her to some extent, however.

Angela does pay attention to her schoolwork but doing that work in front of the television every night is not the best place to do the work. She seems to do most of what she is told to do, but is not told to do much, so she can do mostly what she pleases to do. Although a number of the characteristics of the homes of high achievers are present here, some are missing. This young lady wants to do well, wants to be involved in other activities, listens to discussions about college in her home, and is focused upon her schoolwork, even if she is sometimes distracted. Her mother seems to be missing too often and when at home is not involved enough with Angela. But Angela is responsible, disciplined, involved in extracurricular activities, appears to be internally controlled (she did not need anyone to tell her to do her homework), and her home is relatively quiet and orderly.

Angela seems to be a secure, focused young lady whose home environment, while not perfect, is clearly conducive to higher achievement, and her grades reflect this.

5

SCHOOL PREPARATION AND
THE AVERAGE ACHIEVERS

BRIAN O'CONNER

Brian is a ten-year-old fourth grader who attends the elementary school that serves the poor neighborhood in which many of the poor black and poor Latino Evanston residents live, and that is located next to the middle school attended by most of the students observed for this study. Although he is Latino, he selected the name Brian O'Conner for this work because of his affinity for the actor with that name. The Evanston school system does not give letter grades to students below the level of the sixth grade. This makes it somewhat difficult to compare the academic performance of the students observed who are at that level, such as Brian. For the last grading period, however, he was performing at grade level in math (with one exception), science, and social studies, although not above grade level in any facet of these subjects. His teacher noted in a written assessment that he needs improvement with reading, lacks motivation, often fails to complete his homework, but that he has "considerable potential," a "sharp mind," and is a "very bright" student.

It appears that Brian, while bright, might not be receiving the kind of guidance, discipline, and help with his motivation that often properly comes from the home. His mother has lived in Evanston for eleven years, and his father for twelve years. Both are from Mexico, and they have lived in their present home for three years. They live with their four children, and Ms. O'Conner is a thirty-four-year-old buser at a restaurant. His father is a stocker at a grocery store, which makes this family fairly unusual among the Latino families I have observed over the past several years, given that the mother does work outside the home. Ms. O'Conner completed the sixth grade in school, and her husband the twelfth grade.

Ms. O'Connor believes that Brian's education is very important, as does almost every parent, and encourages him to do well by being aware of his schoolwork, talking about education, and telling him that education is the key to his doing better than either she or his father. She says that she visits his school eight to ten times a year and that she is active in the PTA. She is "glad" when she visits because then she is aware of what is going on at the school. She worries about finding the money to pay for Brian's education after public school, is unaware of any attempts by other students to stop him from doing well, does not believe that discrimination plays a role in her life, and believes that discipline is very important in raising Brian. She was raised on a ranch and began working at twelve years old. She does not ever read a newspaper, and neither she nor her husband read books.

Brian most likes math in school, likes science the least, and thinks that he is doing "fair" in school. To him school is "sort of important," which does not suggest a high value placed upon education. He is, however, only ten years old. No other student has tried to prevent him from doing well in school, so despite what Ogbu (2003) and others have reported about the peer pressure upon nonwhites to do poorly in school, I see very little evidence of this when students or parents are questioned about such pressure. While I believe that the pressure is logical, I find little empirical support for its existence. Although it is possible that parents and students are unaware of the pressure or that it exists mainly for higher-achieving black and Latino students, the reality is that the students about whom I have written thus far have, for the most part, not noticed such a tendency.

Brian says that he devotes an hour a day during the week to his homework, and no time on the weekend. He does not know how far he would like to go in school, but sees no obstacles in the way of his education. He reads a newspaper about once a week, depending upon when his father brings one home, and believes that going to college is the most important thing in his life—so perhaps he does know how far he would like to go in terms of education, given the importance of college in his life. When asked whether race or discrimination played a role in his life, he responded, "Most are Americans," and that he and his friend are the only Mexicans. I assume that he referred to either his school or, more likely, his classroom. It is also noteworthy that he sees himself as Mexican and not American.

Brian says that the language barrier prevents his parents from helping much with his homework because they cannot comprehend the work. He would not change a thing about his family life, and if he could be anyone else it would be Johnny Depp because of his role in the movie *Pirates of the Caribbean*. He appears to be a well-adjusted young man who is not very focused upon education, but he is, according to his teacher, a bright, if undisciplined, young man, despite the importance placed upon discipline by his mother.

The O'Connor family, which includes the two parents, Brian, and two younger brothers, live in a three-bedroom home in which Spanish is the language most often spoken. During the first visit, Brian sat at the kitchen table doing his homework while one of his brothers played close to him, and his mother often told the younger brother to stop the noise because Brian was doing his homework. Ms. O'Connor offered Brian no assistance with the work, but given that she apparently does not speak English and the work is in English, there is little that she can offer. After about twenty minutes of math homework, Brian began to play with one of his brothers, despite the admonitions of their mother. After a time, Brian returned to his homework while Ms. O'Connor told him how important education is if he is to avoid working at a restaurant or supermarket like his parents. She explained to the observer that Brian's grades are not very good and that she would like him to be more responsible about homework and studying.

Although Ms. O'Connor may be limited in the help that she can offer in terms of homework, she probably could help him to become more responsible. She could encourage and support involvement in extracurricular activities, make certain that she asks about the work, or ensure that he is assigned household chores, each of which promotes a sense of responsibility. Brian alternately played and did homework, which is not the best way to do well on the work, until other family members arrived with several children. He then forgot the homework and began to play with his relatives. Brian and his younger brother began to wrestle soon after the observer arrived for the next observation, with Brian explaining how he watches wrestling on the television about twice a week. When the one-and-a-half-year-old brother awakened from his nap, he also wanted to wrestle. Ms. O'Conner told the observer that the baby often takes a swing at her when she asks him to do things he does not want to do, and she believes that this is because he watches his brothers wrestling.

After half an hour, Ms. O'Conner yelled at the boys to stop the commotion, but they paid little attention to her request. When asked by the observer about homework, Brian told her that he would attend to it after dinner. Ms. O'Conner noticed that Brian's jeans were wet and asked him to change them, but he ignored his mother again, and told her that he wanted dinner. After he finished dinner (playing with his brother the entire time), he began to watch the television and to play with his brother again. He did not get around to the homework.

When the observer arrived for the next visit, Brian was not at home, and his mother explained that she had forgotten to tell him to come home after school rather than to go to Family Focus. She then went to get him, but when he arrived he took his time coming into the house. Ms. O'Conner "yells" at him to come into the living room to tell the observer about his day, but he told his mother that he did not want to do so. Ms. O'Conner explained to the observer that Brian was not at Family Focus when she arrived. He had left without permission to visit the home of a friend, which is where she had driven to find him. She was upset that he had done this without calling her and then had lied about it. As a result, he was to be denied the use of his video games. This caused him to loudly complain. The observer noted that while she waited for Ms. O'Conner and Brian to arrive, his younger brother brought out two books in Spanish and started to read, but he became distracted when his cousin tried to take the books away. This continued after Brian arrived and the noise level was "pretty high." By that time, Brian was sulking because he did not want to do any homework and because he had been denied the use of his video games. This lasted only a short time before he began to play with his brother and cousin.

When Ms. O'Conner called the boys to the dinner table, they took their time, and played throughout dinner. Their mother then told them to go to the living room so that she could feed the youngest brother, and Brian started to connect his video game. When his mother noticed this, she told him to put the game away. Again, no homework was done. Neither was any done during the next visit. During that visit Brian was trying to repair his Game Boy, and as he became more frustrated, he began to curse. Ms. O'Conner was at the school at a conference concerning the younger brother. When she arrived, she told the observer that the younger student would have to attend summer school in large part because he has difficulty reading English. The observer noted that the house was in "extreme disarray."

When she arrived for the last visit, the observer noted that Brian was in his yard playing ball. When asked about his homework, he again told the observer that he would do it after dinner, and a bit later when his brother arrived, they played together for a time. In fact, when Ms. O'Conner called them in for dinner, they continued to play for another twenty minutes. As was often the case, Brian and his brother argued and played throughout the dinner. When the brother told the observer that his bicycle had been stolen from the yard, Ms. O'Conner told him that it was his fault for leaving the bike unattended, and Brian told him that he was a dummy for doing so. Ms. O'Conner said nothing about this. This time, however, Brian did start homework, showing the observer a book that he was supposed to read for twenty minutes a day, but which the observer had yet to see him read. He did not read it long before he started to wrestle with his brothers on the floor. Ms. O'Conner told him to do his homework or he would not be allowed to play with his video games, and began to tell the observer that the middle brother had difficulty reading English.

At no time during the observations did Ms. O'Conner help with any of Brian's homework, but Brian did almost no homework. At no time did she ask about his school day. As Tapia (2000) correctly points out, helping with schoolwork is crucial to the child's academic success. The home environment was noisy and unstructured, and Ms. O'Conner did little to teach or enforce discipline, delayed gratification, or internal control in her sons that we could see. Brian was not involved in doing household chores or the kind of extracurricular activities that have been shown to encourage responsibility, discipline, or high self-esteem, all of which are very important for educational success.

In other words, the characteristics of the homes, the parents, and the students who are high achievers were for the most part not present in the O'Conner home, and Brian O'Conner is not a high achiever. On the other hand, he is, according to his teacher "a very bright student who lacks motivation." That motivation and the other characteristics that seem to go with high achievement should begin in the home. It could well be that Brian does as well as he does in school because he is bright. It is not clear, however, how far this brightness can carry him as school becomes more difficult and complex.

Ms. O'Conner, like almost all of the Latino mothers whom I have observed, seems very much to want her children to do well, but she does not appear to understand just what she must do in order to maximize the chances of this occurring. I would also point out that Mr. O'Conner was not a presence at all. In my previous work on poor Latino students (2002), I observed that the boys were often allowed to do much of what they wanted to do, while the girls were under somewhat tighter controls by their parents. The O'Conner boys certainly did much of what they wanted; although their mother was home with them, it should be noted that she works full time as well, and is raising a one-and-a-half-year-old. This is a lot for one parent.

ARACELI ERICA WHITE

Araceli is an eleven-year-old fourth grader at an elementary school that is not located in the neighborhood in which the vast majority of the students observed live. She is at grade-level standards in most areas of reading, writing, math, science, and social studies, but is below in some areas, and according to her teacher is "improving academically," and needs to read for thirty minutes every night. She needs to work on her fluency, and needs one-on-one work in math with the teacher. Araceli appears to be an average student overall.

She lives with her thirty-two-year-old mother, a four-year-old sister, a kindergarten-aged sister, her grandmother, and her mother's boyfriend. Ms. White is from Mexico, has never been married, and has lived in Evanston for five years. She works full time at a child-care facility, and her boyfriend works full time in a plumbing shop. Her boyfriend is from El Salvador and did not complete high school. She did complete high school and attended one year at a university in Mexico. She says that Araceli's education is very important to her because she wants her daughter to attend a university to become a lawyer, a teacher, or some other professional. She tries to encourage Araceli in school by explaining about homework and behaving in class. She sometimes calls the social worker to see how Araceli is doing in school, and visits the school six or seven times a year.

When she visits the school, she is "sometimes happy and sometimes sad," because she does not know what happens in the school. According to her, Araceli sometimes verbally "fights" her teacher. Through second grade, Araceli attended the same school attended by Brian O'Conner, which is next door to the middle school that serves the bulk of the students from the neighborhood in which most poor blacks and Latinos live in Evanston. Ms. White believes that the principal at Araceli's current school has helped her, and she feels "comfortable" there. She thinks that money could later stand in her daughter's way in terms of getting a good education, and that "sometimes" other children try to prevent Araceli from doing well in school. Araceli says that other students "try to distract me" and try to get her in trouble, but she does not know why. She mentions one "troublemaker" by name. Ms. White does not believe that discrimination plays a role in her life, but noted that it did so for her daughter and for African American students at her previous school. This is why she transferred Araceli to the current school

Ms. White was raised in a fairly large family in Mexico and was taught by her mother to be friendly toward others. She tries to teach Araceli to be friendly as well and to follow the orders of adults. She tells Araceli "maybe if you keep going like this with good report cards, maybe the government will get you to college." It appears that at this point she has a somewhat inflated notion of Araceli's academic success. She does not read the newspaper much because she has trouble with English, but her boyfriend helps her with the English "a little bit." She is a " busy mother," working full time, raising three daughters, and volunteering at Family Focus.

As for Araceli, she most likes her art class and her homework about school and believes that she is doing very well in school. School is very important to her because "it gets you ready for what you have to do in the future." She mentioned that she might want to become a zoologist, suggesting high aspirations. Araceli says that she devotes about fifteen minutes a day to homework, that thirty-five minutes is the longest time she has devoted to homework, and that she does her work as soon as she gets either to Family Focus or home. She expects to receive a PhD and sees no obstacles in her way. I suspect that not many fourth graders expect to receive a PhD, and this again speaks to her high educational aspirations.

Araceli says that she reads a newspaper seven times a week, and that her family and school are the most important things in her life. Racial discrimination is not important to her, and both her grandmother and mother help her with her homework, with her mother and her "dad" (the boyfriend helping "every day"). The grandmother is, by the way, the mother of the boyfriend. Araceli notes that her grandmother helps when her mother and "dad" do not understand the work. Again, the Latino parents are very limited in the amount of help they can offer if they do not really understand English, though it was not clear whether Araceli meant understanding of the language or of the work itself. Knowledge of the work on the part of the parent is less important than the child's understanding that the parent thinks that the work is sufficiently important that he or she devoted precious time to help the child. This sends a powerful message to the child about the importance of the schoolwork.

Asked who she would be if she could be any one person in the world, Araceli answered that she would be herself, suggesting some measure of confidence and high self-esteem, and she would not change a thing about her life. Araceli lives on the second floor of a modest two-story house and her "grandmother" lives on the first floor. The observer described the home as "neat and organized," and Araceli and her two sisters were happy to meet the observer. The four-year-old told the observer that it was her job to bring the clean laundry from the basement, and when asked by her mother when it would be convenient for the observer to meet next with them, Araceli pulled out a typed monthly schedule to check on available dates. It appears that she is a well-organized young lady.

At the time of the next visit, the television was tuned to a Spanish-language station and rather loud. While Ms. White folded laundry, Araceli did homework for "about five minutes" while the observer was present. She sat on a sofa and occasionally looked up at the television, and Ms. White did not offer any help or ask about the work. After completing the homework, Araceli made juice from a powdered mix for her sister Jackie, the kindergarten student, and the observer. When her other sister complained that she had no juice, Araceli made juice for her as well. Jackie asked the observer to read *Pocahontas* to her, and a bit later they decided to watch a video of Pocahontas on the VCR. Later, Ms. White came in and reminded the older girls that they were to be in a commercial filmed at Family Focus, and gave them instructions on how to behave and to listen during the taping. Ms. White appears to consider discipline important for Araceli, and Araceli appears to be a responsible young lady.

The observer noted that the television remained on the entire time of the next visit, and that she realized that Ms. White does not own a car. Araceli owns a fish tank, and as Ms. White took out a recently purchased filter for the tank, she explained to the observer that the filter had cost $2, which Araceli now owed her, given that it was her tank. This was perhaps a small lesson in responsibility for Araceli. After the filter was changed, Araceli began her homework, again with the television on, and again with no input from her mother. She did, however, interrupt the work several times to answer questions from Jackie, who was seated next to her at the dining room table.

During the next visit, Ms. White several times asked for and received Araceli's help while baking a cake. When not helping her mother, she was working on two "Mexican-themed" workbooks, and was apparently not happy to be distracted by the talking between the observer and Ms. White. The next time the observer arrived, the television was again on, and Ms. White and Araceli were organizing the living and dining rooms, explaining that they were somewhat messy because they had just arrived. Araceli then emptied the trashcans, and offered juice before playing a computer game with the observer. While she played, her sisters drew pictures and wrote letters from the alphabet on paper supplied by the observer.

After a time Araceli began her homework in her bedroom, but stopped again after about five minutes. Jackie had informed the observer on two previous occasions that she was "Student of the Month" in her class, and this day Ms. White had purchased a cake in celebration. This kind of gesture serves to raise the self-esteem of a youngster, and higher self-esteem is very important to academic success. While the family ate the cake, they watched the television. Ms. White's boyfriend came from his mother's flat downstairs for a few minutes. The observer noted that he comes up occasionally but then returns downstairs fairly quickly.

When the observer arrived for the next visit, Araceli informed her that this was the day for parent-teacher conferences and complained that she had spent the day cleaning the house and helping with laundry because she had no classes. Araceli played computer games for the bulk of the afternoon, again with the television on. Araceli complained to the observer that she wished that she could have some "peace and quiet" in her home, while her sisters played and made a fair amount of noise. When Jackie became upset that she could not make the shapes that she wanted on the computer, she began to shout. Ms. White came into the bedroom and told her to be more quiet, which she did. After she left, Araceli left the room to help her mother with something.

Later, the girls (with the help of Ms. White) put on lipstick and their mother and the observer painted their nails. When the youngest girl put on a fair amount of lipstick, her mother indicated that her "father" would disapprove because he does not like the girls to act older than they are. No homework was done and school was not discussed.

This household seems to have a number of the characteristics of the homes of high achievers, though Araceli is not one of them. The discipline is evident, as is a sense of responsibility on the part of Araceli. Some homework is done, though Ms. White does not ask about it or help with it, and Araceli actually spends little time on it. She is, however, in the fourth grade, and it may be that she has relatively little homework to do. The home is orderly and structured, though not particularly quiet. There was no evidence of involvement in extracurricular activities, though Araceli appears to be internally controlled. Ms. White's boyfriend, while a presence, does not appear to be a factor in the raising of the girls, though his ideas about them acting a certain age seem to have some influence. It is interesting to note that these girls are expected to act their age while Kuyo, the poorly performing tenth grader, apparently drinks alcohol in his home. It does seem that the Latino girls are more closely supervised by the adults.

DANNY SMITH

Danny Smith is a ten-year-old fifth-grade black student at one of the elementary schools in Evanston, though not the one that serves the neighborhood in which almost all of the students involved in this research live. He appears to be an average student working at grade level in most areas of reading, writing, math, science, and social studies. He is below grade level in one area of reading, three in writing (of the eight areas), and four in math (of the eleven areas). His teacher notes that he is "trying hard" and "staying focused," but he apparently answers back when reprimanded, though he "seems to want to do the right thing." He is "a good math student, but is inattentive in class."

Danny lives with his single, twenty-nine-year-old mother and is an only child. Ms. Smith has lived in Evanston all of her life, and she and Danny have lived in their current house for two years. Ms. White works full time at the local high school and part time as well. She completed high school and "some college," and believes that Danny's education is very important to her. It appears that all parents believe this, but that they do not all know just how to translate this belief into actions that help their children to do better in school.

Ms. Smith thinks that Danny's education is important because she wants him to be capable of caring for himself, and to avoid being "labeled" as a black male. This is apparently a reference to the negative labels often given to young black males by many in our society. She mentioned extracurricular activities and religion as important in this process. Gutman and McLoyd (2000) note the importance of involvement in both extracurricular activities and religion in the lives of high-achieving poor black students, but thus far we have not seen evidence of this involvement on the part of any of the poor black students observed. We have not observed any real high-achieving students either. Although we have observed a number of students who are doing well or average work, which may well defy the stereotype of the underachieving, poor nonwhite student, we have not seen the students receiving all As and Bs in school.

Danny's mother says that she encourages him to do well in school by working with him during the summer on his maturity, by complimenting him to raise his self-esteem, and by pointing out positive role models. This last effort is noteworthy because of the many poor black young men observed do not have these positive male role models in their homes. This requires special efforts on the part of their mothers, and we have yet to observe such efforts. Ms. Smith picks Danny up from school every day and talks to his teacher once a week. She points out that she wants him to "be his best." She feels "good" when she visits his school, and says that the school has good teachers and a good curriculum. This is the first time that a parent has mentioned the curriculum at all and may suggest more knowledge and attention paid by Ms. Smith.

She likes the teachers, and indicates that while Danny was once immature he has now matured. According to Ms. Smith, Danny has faced peer pressure to do poorly in school and mentions "bad" friends. It is not clear whether Danny has really faced specific pressure from others to perform poorly or has friends who do so and tempt him to follow their lead. As she points out, "It is hard to be a kid nowadays." She does see "pressure from classmates," and it may well be that these classmates urge Danny to behave in ways that promote lower performance. He is an average student with some behavioral problems according to his teacher.

According to Ms. Smith, Danny says that he gets in trouble in school "because I am black," and she believes that race or discrimination is an issue, but not a "really big" issue. Her upbringing was "hard," in part because of her "mother's condition," in part because she had to attend different grade schools, and as one of nine children she did not receive all of the attention that she "needed." There was prejudice in her grade school, and when she moved and changed schools she did better. She raises Danny to be a "God-fearing person," to live to please God. She reads the local newspaper once a week (it is a weekly paper), but does not read the larger papers very often, and reads religious books "all the time." She relies on God, herself, and one close friend when she has a problem.

Danny most likes his teachers and "activities" about his school, and least likes "the rules." He notes that he cannot chew gum in class, and he is not happy about this. He apparently wants to do things that are not allowed. Danny believes that he is doing well in school, and that school is very important to him because it helps him to "learn things," such as respect and safety. He also indicates that someone else has tried to stop him from doing well in school, but says that it was a person who was a "bad influence" who wanted him to go places he should not have gone. He believes that this person "wanted someone else to get in trouble." As a result of his behavior, Danny was suspended from school. This seems to be less a case of a person trying to pressure Danny into poor academic performance than another boy who was troublesome and wanted to involve Danny in the trouble. Danny says that he works on homework for a half an hour every school night, and an hour on the weekend. Although he indicates that he wants to go to college for two years, he is uncertain how far he expects to go in school. He told the observer that he wanted to go to the National Basketball Association to become a pro basketball player after the two years in college. He does not have very high educational aspirations. He does not ever read a newspaper, feels close to no one at his school, and "doesn't really want to think about" race or discrimination. It seems that few poor black parents or poor Latino parents or their children are bothered by race or believe that their race or ethnicity holds them back. In their view, race/ethnicity and discrimination are not factors in their lives.

According to Danny, he receives help "all the time" from his mother and his grandmother, who lives with them. If he could be one person, he would like to be "like God," suggesting the importance of religion in his life. When the observer first met Danny he was at the local high school taking a swimming class. Ms. Smith picked him up and drove home with the observer and her son. When he arrived, Danny went to the kitchen to warm up food apparently prepared by his grandmother while Ms. Smith went to the store. While eating dinner, Danny turned on the television, but when Ms. Smith arrived, she told him immediately to turn it off and begin his homework. According to the observer, she "oversaw him doing his homework" and constantly talked to him about his assignments. This is precisely the type of involvement with the child's schoolwork seen in the homes of high-achieving poor blacks and Latinos, but not seen at all in many instances so far in this research. In fact, Ms. Smith actually helped Danny with his science homework.

When he shifted to his social studies work, he said to his mother "Mom, I spelled 'February' wrong. How do you spell it?" His mother replied, "[Danny], you have a dictionary sitting right next to you. I told you that you need to start using it more often." "Yes, ma'am" was his response. To which she replied, "'Yes, ma'am' is right." Danny appears to not only have the involvement of his mother in his schoolwork, but Ms. Smith clearly tries to teach him discipline. As she tells him to use the dictionary, she also talks to him about the risks of plagiarism.

When Danny becomes distracted by a conversation between the observer and his mother, she includes him in the conversation, but quickly tells him to return to his homework. In fact, she did not allow him to stop the work even to answer the telephone. A bit later, she asked to see Danny's science report, and told him that he could do better, that he had just thrown it together. At 9:15 p.m. Danny had not completed his homework and Ms. Smith told him that he would have to awaken early the next morning to complete the work. In addition, because he was not as far along as she would like with his science project, he would have to skip swimming the next day to do more work on the project. She seems to demand discipline, responsibility, and attention to his homework from Danny. He is involved in at least one extracurricular activity and apparently in his church as well. These are, as I have indicated, all characteristics of high-achieving poor black students. Danny is, however, not a high achiever. Still, some of the necessary characteristics seem to be in place in his home.

Danny's home is small, neat, and quiet. There is some peeling paint and the furniture is old. The atmosphere, quiet and orderly, is just what is needed, though, to foster higher achievement. Danny's grandmother greeted the observer at the time of the next visit, which occurred on a day off from school for Danny. She asked Danny about his homework as soon as he came downstairs to greet the observer. He replied that he had none because his choir was going on a field trip to sing at the high school. Danny then went to his room to fold and organize some clothes before turning the television on for about ten minutes. His mother arrived and reprimanded him about something on his shirt before talking with the observer about how her job, church activities, Danny's extracurricular activities, and her new business venture kept her very busy.

When Danny returned from his bedroom, she too asked him about his homework, to which he gave the same reply that he had given to his grandmother. When pressed about homework for a different day, Danny said that he had been working on the social studies worksheet and that he would complete the work after swimming lessons, to which his mother replied, "You shouldn't wait until the last minute." When Danny came back downstairs from his room ready to go to his swimming lesson, his mother asked him if he had eaten. When he told her that he had not, she replied, "It will have to wait then, won't it." Ms. Smith does not seem to accept much opposition from Danny.

When the observer next arrived, Danny's grandmother let him in and called up to him to come downstairs. Although the television was on when the observer arrived, the grandmother turned it off when Danny began his homework, which this time was math. After the work, he went to pack his bag in preparation for his swimming lesson. His grandmother told him to empty out the laundry bag and to put his clean clothes away. When he had emptied out the bag, he returned to begin to read a book assigned for one of his classes, and his grandmother suggested that he read aloud so that she could help him if needed. He occasionally did ask her for help. When Danny completed that assignment, he showed the observer a book that he was reading for a contest at his school.

When the observer arrived for the next visit, Danny came downstairs to greet him, and was immediately asked by his grandmother about his homework. He told her that he had completed the assignment, a five-paragraph social studies paper, and was preparing to write a final draft.

It appears that both Ms. Smith and her mother consistently not only ask Danny about his homework, but that Ms. Smith also involves herself in the work. Danny seems to begin his homework soon after he arrives from school or swimming lessons, and pays attention to the work until it is complete. When Ms. Smith arrived home, she asked Danny to clean up his clothes that were scattered about the family room, but not until after he had completed his homework. When he had completed the assignment, she asked to see it, and was critical of the final paragraph telling him that it was not his best effort. Although he was upset at the criticism, she continued to explain that he needed to do better and at one point told him that the work was "C work" and that he was capable of "A work." So, she is involved in his schoolwork, has high expectations of him, and seems to pay attention to his self-esteem. This is a combination not seen in any of the other families observed. Still, Danny's grades do not reflect the reality of the preparation for school that he seems to receive at home. Perhaps this will change as he proceeds past the fifth grade, or perhaps he lacks the motivation needed to do better. It is hard to believe the latter, given the discipline and encouragement provided by his mother.

When Danny had rewritten the paragraph, Ms. Smith told him that this was a better version, but that she believed that he could do better still, that this effort was a B effort and asking "Do you want the B or the A?" Although Danny was late for swimming, Ms. Smith required that he finish the homework before leaving.

When the observer arrived for the next visit, Danny was again working on his homework in his mother's room. He later went upstairs and both did homework and watched the television. In fact, according to the observer, Danny did the homework only during commercials. His grandmother was downstairs and his mother was still at work so no one was there to supervise his work. While his grandmother left to pick up his mother from work, Danny went next door to a cousin's house to retrieve a textbook. The three arrived together and Ms. Smith was upset with Danny, telling him to "find a book soon." After a discussion with three cousins about the location of the book, it was determined that Danny had left it at school in his locker. All four of them received a lecture from Ms. Smith on the importance of being prepared for school in the morning.

When the cousins left, Ms. Smith told Danny, "I'll be honest, [Danny], I am hard on you. But I'm hard on you because I know you can do it. I expect more of you now." She then examined Danny's social studies homework, but because he was not finished with the work, he would not be going swimming. She went over the work in detail, asking at one point, "Does this make sense?" When Danny replied, "No," they worked on the assignment together until he had come up with an "adult" answer on the assignment. Then she checked his math homework and told him to prepare to go swimming.

After dropping Danny off, Ms. Smith explained to the observer that she had attended parent-teacher conferences the previous day, that she and the teacher had agreed that Danny lacked "focus," and that this was a recurring problem. She noted that Danny was the youngest in his class, which may lead to maturity problems. His teacher disagreed with her assessment and concluded that Danny had succumbed to peer pressure to be "cool" and to be funny in class. Ms. Smith, while understanding, still found this unacceptable.

Clearly, Ms. Smith is very much involved in preparing Danny for the educational experience. In fact, many of the characteristics of the family life of high-achieving students are in place in his home. It may well be that the peer pressure to be "cool," which often means to underachieve among many poor urban black and Latino males, has negatively affected him. I have indicated before in this work that I had seen little real evidence of this pressure about which Ogbu (2003) writes so forcefully. The pressure to avoid speaking "standard English," against "being smart during lessons," and against paying attention during lessons—all of which may be (according to Ogbu) interpreted as "acting white"— may well result in poor grades. This seems to be the case with Danny. For the most part, few of the students whom I have observed have indicated that they have experienced this pressure, and it has not seemed to adversely affect performance in any event.

Although some students have indicated that they have experienced this peer pressure, either their grades remained high (Sampson 2002) or their home environments could help to explain the lower grades. In the case of Danny Smith, the home environment would lead us to expect higher achievement than he has shown—so the peer-pressure argument makes sense. Remember that Danny himself indicated in his answers to our questions that he has experienced pressure to "get in trouble." Perhaps the pressure is more "effective" for younger students than for those who are somewhat more mature. If Danny's teacher can see this pressure, and Danny can feel it, we can assume that it is present and has affected him and his performance. Doing the right things at home to prepare a student for school might not be enough if pressure from peers to underachieve is present and effective. However, doing these things is clearly necessary if not sufficient.

REI-REI BARKI

Rei-Rei Barki is a ten-year-old fifth grader at the elementary school outside of the neighborhood in which the bulk of the families live; the school is attended by several of the students observed, including Danny Smith. She is performing at grade level in most areas of language arts, science, and social studies, but below grade level in five of the relevant ten areas of math. Overall, she appears to be about average. She lives with her paternal grandparents and her uncle, who has lived in Evanston for twenty-seven years and in the same house for fourteen years. She is the only child in the house. Her grandfather is retired and worked for a neighboring community. Her uncle, who completed the questionnaire, indicated that he had completed high school, and says that Rei-Rei's education is "very" important because he wants her "to be able to take care of herself financially and go places and get a job." He encourages her to do well in school by placing her in early-bird math before school and during lunch, and by purchasing a computer for her.

He attends her school two or three times a year and feels "good" when he attends, in part because, according to him, the teachers "always have good stuff to say about her." He sees no attempts to prevent Rei-Rei from doing well in school, and believes that race and/or discrimination "sometimes" play a role in his life, particularly when he is walking in stores. Rei-Rei is raised to believe that "love is important," to accept responsibility, and to respect herself and others. He says that he reads a paper every day, and relies on his mother when he has a problem.

When asked what she most likes about school, Rei-Rei responds, "Recess, math, Family Focus, and basketball." It is perhaps telling that three of the four areas mentioned have nothing to do with academics and little directly with school, and the other area mentioned is her weakest subject. She least likes the dirty bathrooms, and believes that she is doing "well" in school. School is very important to her because "You need it to go on in life" and, like her uncle, she does not believe that others have tried to prevent her from doing well.

Rei-Rei says that she devotes ten to twenty minutes a day on homework, which does not seem like very much time, and would like to go to college. She sees no obstacles in her way, never reads a paper, and she thinks that family is the most important thing in her life. She felt close to her third-grade teacher because "she was very helpful and understanding and she was cool to hang out with." She does not think about race and does not get much help, according to her, from family members with her schoolwork. She says that she gets her work done at Family Focus. My observations in the past (Sampson 2002) suggest that few students manage to get much work done at Family Focus after school, in part because the students are arranged in groups and some members of the groups prefer to devote their time to playing and disrupting others. If she could change one thing about her family, it would be to make it smaller, and if she could be any person in the world, that person would be Beyonce. Clearly, Beyonce appeals to the young black girls!

The observer met with Rei-Rei the first time at Family Focus, where, according to Rei-Rei, she goes every day after school. Her uncle picked them up and drove them to her home, where she proceeded to play video games and listen to the radio. She explained to the observer that she generally did her homework at Family Focus so that she can relax when she arrives home. However, the observer saw her do no homework during the time at Family Focus when she and Rei-Rei awaited the arrival of her uncle. While in her bedroom listening to the music, Rei-Rei explained to the observer that she had recently gotten into trouble in school for passing notes and as a result had been grounded at home. She also indicated that she was on the school basketball team, which practiced on Wednesdays and Fridays and played games on Saturdays, which represents evidence of discipline at home and involvement in an extracurricular activity. Rei-Rei indicated that her coach gives her positive reinforcement by telling her when she makes a good pass or a good play. Of course, boosting self-esteem is one of the things that involvement in extracurricular activities can accomplish, which is one of the reasons why it is so often associated with high academic achievement.

Rei-Rei explained to the observer that she had siblings who live with her mother and that she had for a time lived with her father in another state. Her grandmother works full time and her grandfather "works all day long." He watched the television throughout the first visit.

Rei-Rei was not seen doing any homework when the observer next met her at Family Focus. When they went outside to await the uncle, several other children were playing in the snow, and one of the girls told Rei-Rei that another girl "gives head for a dollar" (that is, she performs oral sex for a dollar). All of the children were twelve years old or younger. The girl who was talking to Rei-Rei asked the observer, "Are you ghetto?" only to have Rei-Rei tell her, "No, she's not ghetto."

When Rei-Rei, the observer, and her uncle arrived at her house, Rei-Rei informed the observer that she intended to watch television that evening. They watched videos until the observer left. When the observer next met Rei-Rei at Family Focus, she was playing a game with one of the staff members, as opposed to doing the homework that she said she always does at Family Focus. When they arrived at Rei-Rei's home, she proceeded to her bedroom and, as usual, played video games and listened to music while telling the observer that she sang in a choir at school.

During the next visit, Rei-Rei again listened to music in her bedroom while talking to the observer about a magazine. She did no homework and her only mention of school involved telling the observer that while she was supposed to use an organizer to keep track of homework assignments, she did not see the need for it. The last visit began at Family Focus, and as usual, Rei-Rei was doing no schoolwork. This time she was playing in the gym with other young girls. When they arrived at her home, she again listened to music. This time she also played board games.

In reality, Rei-Rei was not seen doing homework at any time during our visits, either at Family Focus or at home. No member of her family mentioned school at any time, and she appeared to have limited contact with family members. It almost appears that she is raising herself. She did no housework, clearly did not delay gratification, demonstrated no interest in education, and did as she pleased at home. There was noise in her room at all times, and there was no effort on the part of any adult to turn her attention to her academic work. Rei-Rei appears to be a thoughtful young girl who pays minimal attention to school as an academic institution and more to it as a social institution. Her grandmother works at night and was seen only once during our visits, while her grandfather kept to himself. Her uncle works full time and does another job out of the home, so he too is very busy. The family seems to be loving, but few of the characteristics of high-achieving students are present in this home.

AMBER FOSTER

Amber is a twelve-year-old eighth grader at a private school just outside of Evanston. She lives with her mother in a community north of

Evanston, and her family has lived in their current house for one year, after living in Evanston for twenty-four years. She received a B- grade in prealgebra, a C- in history, a C+ in French, a C in English, an A in gym, a B- in life science, and an A- in speech/drama. Thus, in her base courses she is an average student. One of her teachers noted, "She does not give the lesson her full attention" and is sometimes "unsure of what I am asking." Another noted that she had "improved a great deal," while another pointed out that she "had some difficulties this quarter" and that "It will be difficult for her to continue in the second semester if she does not prepare more thoroughly for tests and quizzes."

Her mother, the head of the household, is unemployed, and is either separated or divorced from her husband. She completed high school, and believes that Amber's education is very important to her because of her "future," "reaching full potential," and her "independence." She says that she tries to encourage Amber by talking about her grades, helping her with her homework, and interacting with her teachers and principal. According to Ms. Foster, she visits Amber's school "weekly" and feels "comfortable and accepted" when she does so. Ms. Foster says that the principal and teachers are accessible and accommodating. When asked whether anything stands in Amber's way in terms of her education, she replied that a "lack of focus" and "[Amber] herself" did so. She does not believe that race or discrimination plays any role in her life. She grew up in a large family in which her father was not always present due to "economics," and she was "independent" and "self-motivated."

She raises Amber to believe that "values and morals are important," "to develop her own sense of being," to understand "boundaries and limitations," and "to respect yourself and others." Ms. Foster reads a newspaper once a week and about six books a year. She relies upon herself when she has a problem. She appears to be an independent, confident woman who knows what she wants.

For her part, Amber most likes sports about school and least likes history. She thinks that she is doing fair in school, which is an accurate assessment, and thinks that education is important to her because she needs an education to get a job. No other student has tried to prevent her from doing well in school, and she says that she devotes one and a half to two hours a day to homework, which (compared to the other students observed) seems to be a lot of time, assuming that she is telling the truth. Amber wants a bachelor's degree and sees no obstacles in her way. Her niece is the most important thing in her life and she does not feel close to any of her teachers. She notes that race and discrimination are sometimes issues for her because she lives in a white neighborhood.

Amber receives "a lot" of help with her schoolwork from her mother "whenever" she asks for it, and thinks that this is too much help for her. If she could change anything about her life, it would be for her parents to "get back together," and if she could be any other person, it would be tennis star Venus Williams because she wants to be good at tennis.

"It was funny to see how her entire demeanor changed as soon as her mother left the room. When [her mother] was present, [Amber] was very quiet, reserved, and a bit timid at times. As soon as her mother closed the door, a whole new person emerged." So wrote the observer after her first visit to the Foster home. It appears that Ms. Foster exerts an influence upon her daughter that she opposes in private, and we therefore need to be somewhat careful when analyzing her role in the preparation of her daughter for school. Indeed, Amber apparently attempted to contact the observer on several occasions after the completion of the research without the knowledge of her mother. When Ms. Foster discovered this, she took measures designed to make this more difficult.

As soon as Ms. Foster left the room during that first visit, Amber turned on her computer game and told the observer that she had no homework to do. When asked about an index card on the wall that indicated that her school goals for the year were to make all As and to be more consistent with her homework, she told the observer "It's something that my mom made me do." Although parents should indeed attempt to get students to understand the importance of school and of higher achievement, it is also important that the children themselves support these efforts and accept them as worthy. Otherwise, they will likely be in conflict with the parent, and this helps neither the student nor academic achievement.

When asked about her school life, Amber indicated that she "hates" the racial make-up of the school. There are only a handful of black students in the private school, and this makes Amber uncomfortable. She does, however, enjoy playing sports at the school, which suggests that she is involved in extracurricular activities. In fact, she invited the observer to her basketball game that weekend. She also dislikes living in the all-white neighborhood to which she, her mother, and her stepfather had moved a year earlier. Her parents were involved in a divorce and were separated at the time of the observations.

As soon as Amber heard her mother's footsteps, she "quickly" turned the computer off and opened a science book. When Ms. Foster asked whether she had completed her homework, she told her that she still had to finish "math stuff and I'm done." Ms. Foster indicated to the observer that Amber's lack of focus was a concern for her, telling Amber that she must focus on her schoolwork if she expects to make it to college. When her mother left the room again, Amber asked the observer whether she would like to watch a movie. When the observer pointed out that she had yet to complete the homework, Amber ignored this and proceeded to the living room to turn on the television but when her mother realized that the television was on, she scolded Amber for turning it on. Amber then returned to her room to complete her homework.

During the next visit, Amber told the observer that she had completed her homework, but that she had a take-home test to complete. When Ms. Foster asked about the test, Amber told her that she had completed it, but she privately indicated to the observer that this was not the case. However, the observer noted after seeing tests and quizzes with "very high grades" on the refrigerator that Amber "must have a special gift for learning." During this visit, Ms. Foster talked on the telephone for "nearly the entire length" of the visit, while Amber talked with the observer about how much she missed Evanston and played on her computer, which she instantly turned off upon hearing her mother's footsteps. When Ms. Foster asked whether she was finishing her history homework on the computer, she replied, "Yes"—when in fact she was not doing the work at all. She finally began the work a bit later at the urging of the observer, but she also turned on her stereo while she did this work. When Ms. Foster heard the music, she entered the room and "scolds [Amber] for having the stereo on while she is studying." Amber seemed to know better but did this anyway. In fact, Amber commented to the observer that her mother had become quite strict since their move from Evanston.

Amber talked with the observer while working on her schoolwork, telling her about playing tennis with friends and an upcoming tumbling competition. As the observer left the house, she reminded Amber of her homework and Amber told her that she would just do it in the morning before class.

During the next visit, Amber talked with the observer about the popular students at her school until her mother noticed that she had not done much homework and told her to "get a start on that homework," which she did after checking a buddy list on her computer. Amber devoted the rest of the time to her homework. However, during the final observation, Ms. Foster shared Amber's midsemester grades, which were below average, with the observer and openly scolded Amber about how lazy she was, telling her that she wished that she had the money to hire a tutor for her.

As a result of the midsemester grades, Ms. Foster had decided to enforce stricter rules regarding homework and studying, including sitting next to her every evening while she did her homework or studying, commenting "on absolutely everything that she does," and in the process making Amber "nervous and frustrated." At one point, Ms. Foster took the computer keyboard from Amber, deleted a paragraph, and rewrote it herself. As the observer left, she felt "pretty upset and a bit worried about [Amber]."

There appears to be a considerable amount of stress in this household, with Ms. Foster exhibiting a level of rigidity and insensitivity toward Amber that may well stifle her achievement. Although discipline is needed in order for students to perform well in school, it is also important that students accept the discipline and their responsibility as necessary for their own good. This does not seem to be the case in the Foster home. Amber is involved in the kinds of extracurricular activities that promote a sense of responsibility, discipline, and high self-esteem, but her mother not only seemed to do little to support this self-esteem but was also observed engaging in activities and dialogue that could well diminish it. She scolded and criticized Amber in front of the observer, constantly suggested that she was doing the wrong things, and even took over part of her homework from her.

Parental help with schoolwork is helpful, but the atmosphere in which this is done needs to be supportive and cooperative as opposed to confrontational and accusatory. If the parents do not take the time and invest the energy in the process of convincing the student that the preparation activities in which both are engaged will help the child and that the parent is there to help and support, then the discipline and help with schoolwork may well be counterproductive and seen by the child as oppressive. So, at one level, it appears that Ms. Foster is doing some of the requisite things to promote high academic achievement. However, at another level, it seems that she has not worked to attain the buy-in and cooperation of Amber in this effort. It may well be that Amber feels oppressed and as a result rebels to some extent. Her mother seems to be controlling and not mindful of Amber's self-esteem.

NATHAN KENNY

Nathan is a twelve-year-old seventh grader at the same middle school attended by most of the students observed. His grades are average, with an F in science, a D in social studies, a B in math, a B in language arts, and a B in reading for the most recent grading period. He lives with his thirty-year-old mother, who is the head of the household, and three other children in a home in which they have lived for just over a year. His mother has lived in Evanston for over twenty years.

Ms. Kenny works full time as a driver, and believes that Nathan's education is "very important" "because you need your education to get ahead in life and to get a good job." I find it interesting that so many of the poor parents see the relationship between education and a job as opposed to education for the sake of knowledge or self-improvement. For the poor, a job is probably more crucial than self-actualization. On the other hand, several of the poor black parents interviewed several years ago for my first study on this topic (Sampson 2002), when asked why the child's education was important, mentioned reasons other than a job. It would be interesting to see the extent to which the parents of high-achieving poor nonwhites tend to see beyond a job for their children.

It might be that the ability to see a value of education beyond the job is related to higher achievement. Given that I have no real high achievers in this sample, I really cannot examine this possibility, but it may be worth noting for future research on the role of the family in school preparation.

Ms. Kenny says that she encourages her son to do well in school by telling him to keep up his homework and grades, to listen to his teachers, and to be on his best behavior. She visits his school "every once in a while, when needed." She feels "not so bad" when she visits, and when asked whether anything stood in Nathan's way in terms of getting a good education she responded, "Hopefully don't nothing stands in his way of getting his education unless it has to do with his health." She does not believe that any other child has tried to prevent him from doing well. She raises Nathan to respect others, to know right from wrong, and to not be a follower. She reads a newspaper every day, a book "once or twice," and relies upon herself when she has a problem. Ms. Kenny, who completed the twelfth grade, seems to be essentially on her own as she raises her children and works full time, just like many of the poor black women observed.

Nathan most likes math, music, and drama about his school, and least likes science and social studies. He believes that he is doing pretty good or fair in school, so he seems to have an accurate assessment of his standing. Nathan believes that his education is very important "because I want a good job when I get older." Again, the tie to the job market is evident. He does not believe that any other student has tried to prevent him from doing well in school, and says that he devotes from thirty minutes to one hour a day on schoolwork. When asked how far he wants to go in school, he responded, "all the way" and gave the same response to the question about how far he expects to go. It seems as though his educational aspirations are not only ill defined, particularly when compared to students doing well in school, but that they are hazy as well. Apparently, no one is helping him to define and shape his goals. This makes higher achievement problematic.

Nathan never reads a newspaper and thinks that school and his family are the most important things in his life. He does not think much about race or discrimination because he doesn't "really care what people of different race say or think about me." He says that he receives "a lot of help" from his mother with his schoolwork, and this is enough help for him. He would change nothing about his family life, and he would be Robbin Studder if he could become any one else because "He is the best R and B singer that I know, and is a male."

Nathan lives with his mother, aunt, stepfather, great-aunt, and seven other children, including his aunt's three children and a cousin, in a small, cramped, and disheveled home. During the first visit, the observer noted that the house "seemed chaotic" and was "loud." There were "heaps of dirty clothes" on the floor, dried-up tortillas on the living room floor, and a chair turned upside-down on which a one-year-old balanced himself. This is certainly not the quiet, orderly, and structured home that is generally the case among those who are above average academically.

Nathan talked about his interest in music and pointed out that he sang in the church choir. In response to a question from the observer, he indicated that he might like to go to college to learn how to teach music. During this visit, Ms. Kenney remained in her bedroom, but the great-aunt "carried a belt around and spanked the children with it." Nathan did no homework, and spent his time playing a portable hand game when he was not talking with the observer.

During the next visit, Nathan played games on the observer's cell phone, and again did no homework. This time, "the house was messier" than it was during the first visit, and when Nathan's great-aunt was asked whether he had any homework, she indicated that she did not know. Ms. Kenny was not at home, and when the observer asked Nathan about a play for which he had been rehearsing, Nathan told him that he had not rehearsed that evening because his aunt failed to arrive to take him to the rehearsal.

Nathan did no homework during the next visit either, though this time Ms. Kenny was in the home and the house was quieter. Nathan spent his time knitting a pillow cover for his mother. Indeed, at no time did the observer see Nathan do any schoolwork or hear any adult inquire about school, discuss education, or make any attempt to impose discipline or work on the self-esteem of the children present, including Nathan. This is really a sad situation because Nathan does appear to have the ability to do well in school. He received, after all, grades of B in three subjects, and the F in science was a step down from the C he received for the first grading period. However, the only characteristic of high-achieving homes that we saw in his home was his involvement in extracurricular activities. It is unclear whether any adult in the home really pays much attention to his academic life.

SUMMARY

We observed the families of six average achievers—two Latino families and four black families. In both of the Latino families, there appears to be some interest on the part of the parents, particularly the mother, in seeing to it that the child does well in school. However, the parents do not seem to know what to do in order to prepare the children for the educational experience. Araceli White does her homework without prodding, but her mother does not help her with the work, which is in English, while Ms. White speaks Spanish, and the television is typically on while she does this work.

Brian O'Conner, on the other hand, does mostly that which he pleases, with little supervision from a parent. It does appear that the Latino boys have a great deal more latitude than the girls, and that there is less effort on the part of the parents to discipline the boys or to teach them to delay gratification or to be responsible, all of which are crucial to higher academic performance. Neither is involved in extracurricular activities, but this may have a lot to do with the fact that their parents speak Spanish, and this involvement could be difficult for them to understand or support if the information about it is in English.

Danny Smith, one of the poor black boys, is being raised in a household in which most of the characteristics of high-achieving poor nonwhite students appear to be present. By all accounts, he is a bright young man as well. However, it seems that he is giving in to peer pressure to "be cool," which unfortunately has come to mean for many black students (particularly males, I suspect) not doing well in class and paying more attention to fitting in, appearances, and "attitude" than to studies (Ogbu 2003). Amber Foster has a mother who is very concerned about her academic performance and probably in her mind does the right things to prepare her for school. However, she seems controlling in the extreme, and has apparently not helped Amber to buy into the importance of the things that she tries to do. As a result, Amber seems to fight against her mother and her attempts to almost force Amber to do well. If students do not share the parents' vision and support the efforts to prepare them for school, then the efforts are likely to fail at best, and to backfire at worse.

In two of the four black homes, there seems to be little concern with the education of the students and therefore no real effort on the part of the adults to properly prepare them for school. In the other two, the interest and the effort are there, though several of the key characteristics of the higher achieving homes are missing from both. However, there are issues in each that would need to be addressed in order for the students to do better. In one case, the issue is peer pressure; in the other, it is a mother who seems out of touch with her daughter.

In the Latino homes, I believe that the knowledge is lacking, and in the case of the boy, the will is also lacking. In two of the black homes, the interest or concern is lacking, and in the other two, there are other issues to be confronted. Only in Danny Smith's home did we see many of the characteristics of high achievers. The home was orderly and quiet. Ms. Smith made certain that Danny focused on his homework and was disciplined and responsible. His educational aspirations are reasonably high, and Ms. Smith helped with his homework almost daily. He is involved in extracurricular activities, and it is clear that his mother is in charge. He does not rebel against any of this, instead apparently taking it all for granted. Contrast this with Brian O'Conner, who seems to do and say just about what he wants to with little reaction from a parent.

It must also be noted that the father is present in both of the poor Latino homes, though he does not seem to be involved in the upbringing of the children. His presence still means that the mothers should have more time and energy to prepare the children for school, even though one of the mothers worked outside the home. In the four poor black homes, there were no father figures present, and three of the four mothers worked full time, while the other was unemployed. These mothers must bear the complete financial responsibility for the family and attempt to raise the children and to properly prepare them for school. While this is asking a great deal, some manage to do all of the tasks well, while many others do not. I should remind the readers as well that the six students observed here are all average students. Despite the obstacles of poverty, race, ethnicity, language, disinterest on the part of some parents (or grandparents, in the one case), an overbearing mother, and the lack of knowledge of just what to do, they have managed to do reasonably well in school. The same cannot be said, however, for the five students discussed in the next chapter.

6

SCHOOL PREPARATION AND
THE LOW ACHIEVERS

ALMA PEREZ

Alma is a nine-year-old second grader at the elementary school that serves most of the students from the west-side neighborhood in which most of the poor Latino and poor black families in Evanston live. She meets grade-level standards in five of the seven reading categories with some intervention, and is not making satisfactory progress in the other two. In the eight categories of writing, she meets the standards in four categories and needs help in the other four. Alma needs help in three math categories, and is at grade level in five. She needs help in two of the three social studies categories. I consider her to be a below-average student, especially considering that she has had to repeat the second grade, apparently because she was not ready to move on to the third grade.

Her mother, Ms. Perez, is from Mexico and has lived in Evanston for four years. She is thirty years old, has one other child, works full time, and lives with her husband, who is a stacker in a store. Mr. Perez completed the fourth grade in Mexico, while Ms. Perez completed the fifth grade. Like all of the poor parents interviewed, Ms. Perez believes that Alma's education is very important, but unlike most she did not offer any reason for the importance. Most of the poor parents interviewed have tied education to the job market, but Ms. Perez does not. It is as though she believes that education is important but does not know why.

She says that she encourages Alma to do well in school by telling her to put more effort into her schoolwork and to pay attention in school. Ms. Perez visits Alma's school six or seven times a year, and she feels "fine" when she does so. She notes, however, that she has an interpreter when she visits the school, even though she knows "a little English." Ms. Perez says that she feels fine when she visits because "the teacher speaks well to her." It is important that teachers understand that poor parents, particularly those with language issues, may be intimidated by the school environment, by the dress and education of the teachers, and by the articulate manner in which most teachers speak. All of this may well get in the way of parents visiting the school; when they do, they may hamper communication with the parents.

Ms. Perez wants Alma to learn, but points out that she is "easily distracted." She believes that nothing stands in her way of receiving a good education, and does not believe that any other child has tried to stop Alma from doing well in school. Neither race nor discrimination affects them, according to Ms. Perez, and she says of her upbringing that it was "fine" and "boring." She tries to talk to her children, to keep them healthy and in a "good mental state." She reads magazines twice a week and reads to her young son and Alma in Spanish daily, according to her. She relies upon her sister when she has a problem.

When asked what she likes most about her school, Alma replied, "Art, library, and music." She apparently does not particularly like any of the academic areas, but remember that she is only nine years old and perhaps should not yet be expected to like those areas to which she is just being introduced. She least likes the "bad kids," and she believes that she is doing well in school. She apparently does not understand the significance of being held back a year. Alma thinks that her education is important "so [she] can learn," and she thinks that another student has attempted to stop her from doing well by asking her for help during a test, which she says was a hard test. It is not really clear that this was an effort to stop her from doing well so much as another student seeking assistance.

She says that she devotes forty or fifty minutes a day to her homework, that she wants to go to college, and that she expects to do so. She sees no obstacles in her way and wants to go to college to become a teacher. I find it interesting that most of the young people interviewed see few if any obstacles in their way despite their poverty, their race and ethnicity, and existing discrimination, of which they are for the most part unaware. They seem to have a great deal of confidence and high hopes.

Alma notes that she does get a lot of help from her parents with her schoolwork, more from her mother than from her father, and that she needs even more help. She is at least aware of her academic limitations. If she could be any one person in the world, she would be her mother "because I look like her."

Like many of the parents, particularly the poor black parents involved in this research, Ms. Perez typically picks Alma up from Family Focus after she leaves her job. Because almost all of the black mothers work full time, they are not at home when their children leave school. The children walk to Family Focus, where they wait for their parents to pick them up or for the parents to arrive home so that the children can then walk home. The observer met Alma for her first observation at Family Focus and found her working on her homework alone at a desk. Alma immediately asked the observer for help with her math, suggesting that she does in fact want to do well and is aware that she needs help to do so. It is also important to point out that our experience suggests that many of the students who go to Family Focus after school do not devote much of their time to their schoolwork even though Family Focus seems to try to promote this.

Alma then moved on to her English homework, again asking the observer for help, and talking with the observer while working on her assignment. Her older cousin soon entered the room with two friends, and Alma told the observer that she lived downstairs from her cousin's family. When Ms. Perez arrived, she asked the cousin whether Alma had completed her reading. The cousin replied that she had not read with Alma but that her homework was complete. So Ms. Perez checked on the homework, and she apparently expects that someone will read with Alma as well.

After walking the few blocks to the Perez home, Ms. Perez told the observer that Mr. Perez takes the children to school every day and uses his break from work to pick them up and take them to Family Focus. She also notes that Alma is easily distracted and gets into arguments on the school bus. Mr. Perez takes her to Family Focus so that she will not have to ride the bus and get into those arguments. Although Ms. Perez is not certain why Alma "starts" these arguments, she prefers that she not ride the bus.

While the observer talked with Ms. Perez, Alma played with her pet hamster while her brother watched cartoons on the television, which was not turned off—even when Ms. Perez began to read to him in Spanish. Ms. Perez explained that the current second-grade teacher has suggested that Alma read at home, given her problems with reading, and that she has asked a person at Family Focus to help her to read. As noted earlier, many of the Latino parents seem to want very much for their children to do well in school, but often do not know what this entails. They do, however, seem to want to find this out, and are then willing to do that which they must and can do. Of course, this is not the case for all of the families, but there does seem to be a willingness on the part of many to seek help.

The observer met Alma at Family Focus to begin the second visit as well, but this time the students were in an assembly. When that assembly ended, Alma "dashed" out and went to a classroom to begin her homework, while other students "ran around the classroom and yelled," according to the observer. As I have indicated earlier, it is not uncommon for students at Family Focus who are supposed to do their homework in classrooms to do none, but rather to talk and play. This is, however, not the case with Alma. Alma told the observer that she did not talk with the other girls, all of whom were black, because they thought too much of themselves and sang too loudly. All of the young black girls in the room were sitting around a table singing together, but Alma did her homework—even though the environment was not really conducive to doing the work.

Earlier, her older cousin told the observer that Alma always did her homework until five o'clock, and then she went to another room to have an older student help her with her reading. Alma appears to be focused, disciplined, and to know what she needs to do. When Ms. Perez arrived, she asked Alma whether she had completed her homework, again expressing both her interest and concern, and letting Alma know how important she thinks this work is. Ms. Perez also asked Alma whether anyone had read to her, and when she indicated that she had not had the time because of the assembly, Ms. Perez informed her that she would have to do the reading with Alma since it had not been done at Family Focus. When they arrived at the Perez home, Alma ran to the cage in which her two hamsters lived, but Ms. Perez "yelled" and told her that she had to complete the homework, telling her at one point, "finish up so you could read to me and no watching television." When Ms. Perez went into the kitchen, Alma—in response to the urging of her brother—turned the television on to a cartoon channel. Ms. Perez, upon hearing the television, indicated that she was unhappy that the television was on and turned it off herself.

When Alma finished her homework, Ms. Perez asked her to read a book that Alma indicated she had already read. Although Alma indicated her preference for reading a different book, her mother told her to reread the book anyway. Alma said that she wanted to read only the last chapter, but Ms. Perez said that she should start at the beginning. At this point, the television was on again in response to the actions of the younger brother, and it had become a distraction to Alma. Ms. Perez then turned the television off and promised her son that she would turn it back on after Alma completed her reading.

Clearly, Ms. Perez wants to maintain the kind of quiet, orderly home environment that most often characterizes the homes of high-achieving poor nonwhite students. She also makes certain that Alma is responsible, stresses discipline, inquires about Alma's schoolwork, and goes out of her way to make certain that Alma works on that area of her academic work that requires extra help. However, as Alma began to read, she asked Ms. Perez whether a certain word was correct, and Ms. Perez told her to ask the observer, indicating that she felt very badly that she could not help, that she often is not sure that Alma is reading correctly because she cannot read or speak English well enough to teach Alma to read.

In many of the poor Latino households, the mother wants the student to do well, is prepared to help in that effort, but does not know just what to do; if that is the case here, she does know much of what to do, she just does not know how to do it. The language barrier is a major issue here. Ms. Perez tried mightily to press the observer, who speaks both English and Spanish, to help Alma, only to be told repeatedly that she was there only to observe. Alma struggled mightily with the reading, often guessing what a word might be because she could not pronounce it. Ms. Perez believes that Alma was held back a year in school because she could not read and paid little attention. It is difficult for a student to pay attention when she has no idea of what is being said or of its meaning. In the Perez home, it appears that Spanish was the language learned by Alma, and she probably knew little English when she entered school. This put her behind others who already knew English, and would have required a special program in school for students who start knowing no English.

After reading a paragraph, Alma could not summarize the paragraph for the observer because she had no idea what the words meant. While she understands English and speaks the language well, there are many words she does not know. This makes all of her academic work very difficult, and given that her mother neither speaks nor understands much English, she cannot really help her with her schoolwork. She does manage, however, to convey the importance of the work consistently to Alma. As the observer left for the evening, Ms. Perez apologized for not knowing any English and for being unable to help her daughter. She clearly wants to do the right things.

When the observer next arrived at Family Focus, she "saw kids standing, talking, running around, and playing. Sitting at a table was [Alma] with her reading tutor." So, Alma remains focused on her work—even while others are not paying any attention to theirs. In this case, however, her work was reading, and as it became clear that she did not understand many of the words, she became disinterested. When Ms. Perez arrived, they prepared to leave for home. She noticed some colored construction paper in the hall and told the observer that the paper would be useful for Alma because she was responsible for decorating candles for their church, suggesting Alma's involvement in an activity beyond the school and home.

Upon arriving at the home, Alma began her nightly reading, with Ms. Perez telling her young brother to go to another room to avoid distracting Alma. Ms. Perez told the observer this evening that she pays the reading tutor $10 an hour to help Alma. This is a poor family, but they still manage to pay a tutor to try to help their daughter. As I have indicated, they really want to do the right things.

During the next visit, the observer helped Alma to understand the meaning of a particular sentence. After about twenty minutes of explanation on the part of the observer, Alma finally understood. According to the observer, "She was so excited and was jumping in her seat that she understood." After a bit she became tired and wanted to stop, but Ms. Perez told her to continue the reading.

During the next visit to the Perez home, Ms. Perez asked Alma to sit next to her at the kitchen table in order to go over and help her with her schoolwork, to the degree that she could. Alma had to draw several pictures and her mother helped her with the assignment, at several points completing the drawings for Alma. When the drawings were complete, Alma turned her attention to her reading, several times looking to her mother or the observer for help with various words. When Alma indicated that she did not want to read anymore, Ms. Perez told her to read one more page, only to relent when Alma put her head down on the kitchen table.

Alma had only a half-day of school on the day of the next observation, and the observer arrived late that evening, expecting to observe Alma doing something other than reading or schoolwork, given that she had much of the day to do that work. Alas, when the observer arrived, Alma was reading to her mother, with Ms. Perez "angrily" telling her to pay more attention to the reading. At one point when Alma was about to turn a page, her mother yelled at her to tell her what had happened in the story that she had read. Alma was unable to summarize what she had read, and Ms. Perez told her to reread the page, scolding her for looking to the observer for help. Alma responded to the yelling and the scolding by crying, and Ms. Perez was herself crying.

Ms. Perez explained to the observer that Alma's teacher had recommended that Alma be placed in a bilingual education program, but Ms. Perez was uncomfortable with that suggestion, given that Alma does not know how to read or write Spanish, though she can speak the language. Ms. Perez indicated that she is confused about what to do, although she told the observer that she had told Alma that she would be punished until she began to do better in her classes, including math. Her teacher had said that Alma had been caught cheating, and that she only did well on her assignments when working in a group, which allows her to use the work of others. Throughout this conversation, Ms. Perez cried. She explained to the observer that she had given Alma anything she wanted, that she felt badly when she asked Alma to continue to read after Alma indicated that she wanted to stop, but that it was for her own good.

Ms. Perez then asked the observer for her advice on the bilingual education class, only to be told by the observer that this was an issue that was probably best discussed with Mr. Perez and with Alma. It is very clear that Ms. Perez is concerned about how Alma does in school and is prepared to do all that she can do to help her. It is also clear that she does not really know what to do. She provides the kind of home environment that is conducive to higher achievement, provides the necessary discipline and inquiries about the schoolwork, encourages extracurricular activities, and requires Alma to be responsible. However, her inability to read or speak much English and her limited understanding of the American school system limit what she can do to prepare Alma for her education.

Mr. Perez was not seen at all during our seven visits with the family, and it is not clear that he plays much of a role in the upbringing of the two children. It does appear that Ms. Perez bears the responsibility for the school preparation, which is the case in virtually all of the homes of both poor Latinos and poor blacks. Alma is struggling in school, and the inability of her mother to understand English is a large part of the problem. Bilingual education might help, though this is far from clear, but her mother cannot even really understand the advantages and disadvantages of this approach. Apparently, the school system has done little to help the family to deal with this decision.

ALIYAH MAXWELL

Aliyah Maxwell is a thirteen-year-old eighth grader at the middle school that serves the majority of the poor black and poor Latino middle school students who live in the neighborhood in which Family Focus is located. Her grades for the first and second grading periods of this school year indicate that she is a low-achieving student. For the first grading period, she received two grades of F and three Ds in her academic subjects, a B in physical education, and a C in art. For the second marking period, she received three Cs, one D, and one F.

She lives in a house with her mother, who is fifty-one years old, and three other children. Ms. Maxwell has lived in Evanston for forty-nine years, and in her current house for three months. She is single and works as an assistant in a local school. Ms. Maxwell has completed high school, and like all of the other parents observed, she believes that Aliyah's education is very important because "she has to one day fend for herself." Like almost all of the parents interviewed thus far, Ms. Maxwell ties Aliyah's education to a very concrete and economic goal. Ms. Maxwell says that she tries to encourage Aliyah in school by having her bring her tests home and by helping her with her reading and spelling. She visits her school four times a year, but does not like the school or some of the teachers because they "talk rudely to the kids."

Ms. Maxwell believes that Aliyah's teachers and friends stand in the way of her getting a good education. She indicates that Aliyah "always wants to go out and do things with her friends," that she "always wants to spend money." She believes that the teachers try to stop Aliyah from doing well in school, that they are prejudiced, and they "all stick together," that once one of them forms an opinion about Aliyah, they all agree with that opinion. So she apparently thinks that Aliyah's poor grades are a function of the negative opinions of her held by a few teachers. This relieves Aliyah of any responsibility for her achievement and Ms. Maxwell of much responsibility for preparing her.

She thinks that Aliyah's teachers were guilty of racial discrimination last year, "but not this year." She was raised by a strict father who "didn't want us hanging out with the bad crowd . . . wanted us to make something out of ourselves. To be strong. We had chores. We got whippings if we didn't do them." She believes that discipline and punishment are important in raising Aliyah, and that the "word of God" is also very important. She does not allow Aliyah to go out. Ms. Maxwell reads a newspaper twice a week, a book seven days a week, and relies upon God when she has a problem.

Aliyah likes most about her school the principal and least likes the teachers. It is difficult to imagine an eighth grader who does not like her teachers doing well in school. The student does not have to like the teachers, but disliking them is another issue, particularly if your mother dislikes them and blames them for the failures of her daughter, as well. She believes that she is doing fair in school, which seems to be an overestimation of her performance, and like her mother, she thinks that education is very important. She thinks this because she "wants to go to college and become a nurse." So she has reasonably high educational aspirations, but these so far do not match her educational performance at all.

Aliyah does not believe that any other student has tried to prevent her from doing well in school and says that she works on her schoolwork an hour each day. She would like to go to college, expects to do so, and sees no obstacles in her way. She never reads a newspaper and believes that her family is the most important thing in her life. She feels close to one particular eighth-grade teacher because the teacher "inspired me to do things that I did not want to do." Race and discrimination are things about which she thinks because she does not "know why they treat people different." She says that she receives "a lot" of help from her mother with her schoolwork and mentioned that she receives this help "every other day." It is not clear that help every other day is "a lot," particularly when we remember that help with schoolwork by a parent is probably the single best predictor of the academic success of poor nonwhite students.

Aliyah would like for her family to be closer together and to "stop arguing." If she could become any one person in the world, that person would be her mentor "because she is fun and she is a good student."

The Maxwell family lives on the second floor of a single-family home that was converted into a two-family home, located a few minutes from the Family Focus facility. The observer met Aliyah at Family Focus for the first visit, and the two walked together the short distance to the Maxwell home. Ms. Maxwell asked Aliyah what happened at school that day, but Aliyah informed her that nothing had happened. There was no discussion of homework or the specifics of the school day. Ms. Maxwell informed the observer that she had Bible study that evening and complained that the house was cold and that the family might have to move again soon due to the lack of heat. She also complained to the observer that the white teachers at Aliyah's school were prejudiced and "didn't want to see her graduate anyway," and that Aliyah needed to not allow her mouth to get her in trouble at school, particularly given the racial prejudice at the school. It is interesting to note that we have observed over a dozen poor black families with children at this middle school over the last four years and have never before heard this complaint. She repeated this assertion "over and over" to Aliyah.

Given the importance of internal control and a sense of responsibility to educational achievement, it appears that Ms. Maxwell is doing more harm than good with this effort. If Aliyah's performance is determined by the prejudice of her teachers, then not only is the performance out of her hands but she also has no responsibility for it. This limits performance.

Aliyah has a seventeen-year-old brother, a twin brother who was described by Ms. Maxwell as "a brain," and a five-year-old foster brother. The twin brother was observed four years ago for my research and was an average student. It may be that he has blossomed into an outstanding student, but it may also be that his mother exaggerates his ability and performance. I would suspect that it is more the latter than the former. In any event, this comment in front of Aliyah does little to boost her self-esteem.

When the observer arrived for the next observation, Aliyah was still at Family Focus and Ms. Maxwell had not yet arrived from work. Aliyah's twin brother took the observer on a tour of the house. The observer noted that all of the rooms were quite small and messy. Indeed, she wrote of Ms. Maxwell's bedroom, "There were clothes strewn all over the floor, bags, and boxes were everywhere too. There were no dressers or chests of drawers. Ms. [Maxwell's] bedding consisted of a mattress and box spring on the floor." Aliyah arrived soon and told the observer that her room too was "junky." "Clothes were strewn all over the floor" and she too had only a mattress and box spring on the floor. The twin brother's bedroom was too small to be considered a bedroom. Indeed, it contained no bedding.

This information is given to allow the reader some idea of the conditions in which many poor people must live. Still, we expect that the parents in these home will do the things necessary to help their children to do well in school. Many do this despite their living conditions. However, the homes in which the poor students manage to do well in school seem to be quiet, orderly, and structured. These characteristics promote studying and concentration and aid in the process of instilling discipline and responsibility in the students. They have yet to be seen in the Maxwell home.

When Ms. Maxwell arrived from work, she asked Aliyah about school, but did not ask about anything specific. They both sat in the living room with the television on while sorting through photographs. No homework was done, and Ms. Maxwell did not help Aliyah with any.

When the observer next arrived, the television was on again. Aliyah came out of her bedroom to greet the observer and proceeded to watch the television while playing with her cell phone. When Ms. Maxwell arrived, she did not ask either Aliyah or her twin brother anything about school at all. She made a comment about the cost of cell phones and went to her bedroom, while Aliyah spent the rest of the evening watching the television and playing with her new cell phone, apparently a gift from her father. Again, no homework was done, there was no discussion about school or schoolwork, and no household chores were performed.

Aliyah was not at home when the observer arrived for the next visit, and she was apparently still at Family Focus, though according to Ms. Maxwell, she knew that she was supposed to be at home at that time. When Ms. Maxwell called Family Focus to ask about her whereabouts, a staff member told her that Aliyah had left earlier. She then called the home of one of Aliyah's friends only to be told by the friend that Aliyah was not there either, that she was at Family Focus. Upset by this, Ms. Maxwell explained to the observer that she had earlier reprimanded Aliyah for failing to wash the dishes after being told to do so. She went on to explain that the children rarely wash the dishes when told and that she generally ends up doing them herself. This is not the kind of discipline or responsibility seen in the homes of poor nonwhite students who are high achievers.

In fact, Ms. Maxwell said that she believed that Aliyah was indeed at her friend's home and that the friend simply lied at the behest of Aliyah. A few minutes later, Aliyah arrived home. When confronted about her whereabouts, Aliyah maintained that she was indeed at Family Focus, and both she and her mother laughed about the incident. That evening, though, Aliyah did homework for the first time, while sitting on the sofa in the living room watching the television. Again, there was no discussion of school, no chores, no evidence of involvement in extracurricular activities, no effort to raise or support Aliyah's self-esteem, and no quiet home environment.

The next visit was rather short. Aliyah did not have school because of a local holiday. Although Ms. Maxwell asked her whether she had any homework, to which Aliyah replied that she did not, the time was spent watching the television. During the last observation, Ms. Maxwell complained to the observer that her five-year-old foster son had been asked to leave his Head Start program because he would not stop fighting other children, and that she was not prepared to leave her job to care for him. This was said in his presence. She went on to explain that she needed help from his biological mother and grandmother given that she was the only source of support for the four children.

When Aliyah arrived a few minutes later, Ms. Maxwell asked her whether she had any homework, and this time Aliyah indicated that she did. She promptly pulled work from her book bag and began her homework while watching the television. She worked on the schoolwork for an hour and a half with the television on the entire time. Although Ms. Maxwell asked Aliyah about her schoolwork on several occasions, she never required specific answers and never went over the work with her daughter on the few occasions when Aliyah did any work. The television remained on for most of the time that the observer was in the home, there was no real discussion of education or of educational goals, no involvement in extracurricular activities, and Aliyah's "responsibility" for household chores was the subject of laughter. Ms. Maxwell showed none of the kind of encouragement or help for Aliyah that she said she provided in the interview. Aliyah did not show much discipline. Rather, she visited her friend when she was not supposed to do so and apparently lied to her mother about it. In fact, few of the characteristics of the family life of higher achieving poor black and Latino families seemed to be in place here.

ANDRE HILL

Like Aliyah, Andre Hill is a thirteen-year-old eighth grader at the middle school that serves most of the poor students in the neighborhood in which they both live. Although Andre received a B in math, he received a C in social studies, a D in science, an F in language arts, an F in French, and an F in reading. He also received an F in foods and a C in physical education. I consider him a low-achieving student.

Ms. Hill, his mother, has lived in Evanston for twelve years, having grown up in Chicago, and they have been in their current house for three years. She is thirty-one years old, married, and lives with three other children. She works full time in the health care field and has completed two years of college, while Mr. Hill has completed one year of college. She did not indicate whether Mr. Hill worked. Like all mothers, she believes that Andre's education is very important, because she "wants him to graduate really bad," but it was unclear from just what level she wanted him to graduate. She says that she tries to encourage Andre to do well in school by discussing the history of his family with him and by motivating him to be successful. She visits his school "a lot," and when she does she is "sometimes worried," but she did not explain why she feels this way.

Ms. Hill believes that Andre's father's history, drugs, gangs, and friends stand in the way of his getting a good education. These could well be formidable obstacles indeed! She does not think that other students attempt to prevent Andre from doing well in school, and neither does she think that teachers try to limit him. Race or discrimination "never crosses her mind." This is very different from the picture of the teachers at the same school painted by Ms. Maxwell and by many other parents with students at the same school for that matter.

Ms. Hill says that her upbringing was "kinda tough." Her "mom's life made it kinda tough." She thinks that Andre is angry due to her ex-husband, and notes that "he talks back"—that is, he challenges adults during conversation. Ms. Hill rarely reads either a book or a newspaper and relies upon herself when she has a problem.

Andre most likes about his school "the people you hang with" and "being with my friends." This does not sound like a young man with education on his mind. He least likes "class work," and does not like to do homework. He believes that he is doing fair in school, and that education is very important to him because it will allow him to obtain a "better job" and to be a "smarter person." He does not seem at all concerned with his education, and he notes that no other student has tried to prevent him from doing well in school. According to Andre, he devotes twenty minutes a day to homework and wants and expects to go to college. While he sees no obstacles in his way, it seems to me that he is overlooking his own lack of interest in school and his performance.

Andre never reads a newspaper, but neither does his mother, and he says that his mother and family are the most important things in his life. He does not think about race, and says that he gets "a lot" of help from his mother with his schoolwork when he asks, which he does "sometimes." If he could change one thing about his family life, it would be that he be required to do "less chores and housework." Interestingly, these activities are conducive to higher academic performance among poor nonwhites because they promote responsibility and discipline. He would want to be himself if he could be anyone in the world.

The observer met with Ms. Hill at Family Focus to begin the first observation, but Andre had apparently gone to another facility to play basketball. During their conversation, Ms. Hill explained to the observer that Andre had recently been caught stealing from a local store, and she believed that peer pressure was a big factor in his life. In the two cases in which he was caught stealing, his friends had also been involved. She apparently blamed the friends as though Andre had no responsibility for his actions, but she did tell the observer that she wished that Andre had a greater sense of responsibility. The problem is that this is largely her responsibility to instill in her son.

Ms. Hill told the observer that Andre would "lose" notes sent home by his teachers for her to sign, and would also "lose" his homework. After the conversation Andre arrived but stayed only a few minutes before leaving to play basketball. Either Andre is quite irresponsible, or he lies to his mother or both. He was not seen during this observation doing any schoolwork though other students were in classrooms at Family Focus, with a few seen doing schoolwork.

On two occasions when the observer had arranged to meet with the Hills, Ms. Hill was not at her home, and on one of those occasions the observer met with Andre at Family Focus. Andre spent his time talking with friends about basketball and did no homework despite the fact that they were in a classroom in which homework was supposed to be done. Andre did much the same on the third visit as well before he went to play basketball with the others in his group. The observer noted that many of the students waiting to play could have done homework, but that only two out of the twenty students waiting to play did so. The basketball court is not the best place to do the work in any event.

When Ms. Hill arrived to take Andre home, he begged her to allow him to stay and to continue to play ball even though he had not completed his homework and had chores to do at home. She allowed this and left with the observer and two younger children for her home. While at the very small house, Ms. Hill told the observer that Andre's father was a drug user with a very bad temper and that Andre reminded her of his father. She also told the observer that she worried a great deal about Andre before she had to leave to do errands. Andre had yet to arrive home when she and the observer left.

When the observer arrived for the next visit, Andre was not yet home, and his two younger brothers were watching the television in the living room with Ms. Hill's husband. Ms. Hill explained to the observer that basketball seemed to be much more important to Andre than his schoolwork. She did not appear to realize the role that she could play here. She seemed to allow Andre to place basketball above his schoolwork and household chores. She also talked with the observer about college life and told him that she tells Andre how hard it is to obtain a job with a criminal record, suggesting her concern that Andre may someday have such a record.

When Andre arrived home, he began to play a video game and to "talk back to his mother in a manner that I could never even imagine talking to my mother," according to the observer. A bit later, Ms. Hill asked Andre about his homework, to which he replied, "I did almost all of it, except my math." It is difficult to imagine that this was true, given that he seems to spend almost all of his time at Family Focus playing basketball. When questioned about the math homework by Ms. Hill, he replied that he had lost his textbook. Andre continued to play the games.

When his mother yelled at him to do some cleaning in the kitchen, Andre complained that he had to eat dinner first, before finally starting the cleaning. Ten minutes later, he sat down to watch his brothers play games.

The observer next met Andre at Family Focus on the basketball court, before they walked the short distance to Andre's home. When they arrived, Andre again began to play games with his brother. Ms. Hill told the observer that Andre had recently received his report card, which showed several failing grades. When she had asked Andre about the card, he initially told her that he did not know where it was. After an hour of playing games, Andre began to do his homework, but he did so on the floor next to his two brothers who were fighting and playing. During the next twenty minutes, Andre managed to write a heading and a title on a page, while Ms. Hill watched the two younger brothers play video games.

Like many mothers of poor nonwhite students, Ms. Hill seems concerned with Andre's education, but does nothing at all that will help to prepare him for school. There is very little discipline shown, almost no responsibility, and no ability to delay gratification. The home environment is anything but quiet and orderly. Almost no homework is done, and Ms. Hill does not check it or help with it, despite what Andre said in answering the questionnaire. The one extracurricular activity in which Andre participates is not really extracurricular; rather, it is what Andre does most of the time, and he cannot play on the school basketball team due to his low grades. His mother fails to impose order and so, despite her concerns, her son does much of what he wants to do, and he does not want to do school-related work. His grades reflect this.

ADAM BANKS

Adam Banks is another low-achieving black student who attends the same middle school attended by Andre and Aliyah. He is a ten-year-old sixth grader. His grades were an F in language arts, an F in reading, and Ds in social studies, math, and science. He lives with his twenty-six-year-old mother, five other children, and the father, though his mother indicates that she is the head of the house. Ms. Banks is currently unemployed and has lived in Evanston for nine months. She graduated from high school, and believes that Adam's education is "extremely" important; when asked why, she replied, "Personality, right of passage."

Ms. Banks encourages Adam to do well in school by helping with his "organizational skills," his study habits, and his homework, and visits his school several times a year. When she visits the school, she says that she feels "optimistic," and says that this is because she feels that her son can "overcome." It was not made clear just what Adam is to overcome, but Ms. Banks does not appear to be angry or intimidated by the school visits. When asked what stood in Adam's way in terms of receiving a good education, her response was his "attitude," suggesting that Adam may have a negative attitude toward school.

Apparently, no other student has tried to prevent Adam from doing well, and Ms. Banks does not believe that race or discrimination plays a role in her life. She was raised by a single mother with a "single-family income," which suggests that she too was raised in a low-income family. In raising Adam, she says that faith, love, respect, and discipline are stressed. She reads a newspaper daily, a book once a week, and relies upon her mother and God when she has problems.

Adam most likes about his school history and least likes math. He says that the "teachers are okay." He believes that he is doing fair in school, and that his education is very important because he wants to go to college in order to play football. He wants to attend Ohio State University and use that as a stepping-stone to playing professional football. So, at ten years of age, he is pointing toward a professional football career, and college is a stepping-stone to that end. Apparently, he is not so much interested in college for the educational benefit but for the football opportunity. He is, however, only ten years old, so we should perhaps not make too much of this.

Unlike his mother, Adam believes that another student has tried to prevent him from doing well in school. When asked to be specific, he said that some people do not like him, and that they "start things" because "some people just do not like me." This does not seem to mean that a person has tried to limit his academic achievement. He says that he devotes thirty minutes a day to homework, and an hour while at Family Focus. He wants and expects to go to college, and thinks that the only real obstacle for him is that his teachers do not allow him to ask questions. To Adam, his family is the most important thing in his life, and he thinks that there is some discrimination in the classroom, which makes him "angry."

Adam says that he gets a lot of help with his schoolwork from his mother and wishes that he could be Priest Holmes, the professional football player, because he is "a good football player, a good person who works with jail inmates and wants to help others."

Ms. Banks was a single mother at sixteen years of age when she gave birth to Adam, the oldest of six children. Unemployed, she devotes her time to caring for the six, including a three-month-old baby. She is married, but indicated that her husband plays no real role in the family. When the observer arrived at her home, which like most of the others is close to Family Focus, he noted that many young children were "running around," and that "the house was [in] chaos, in the sense of several screaming children running around." The living room contained an old sofa and a small television sitting on the floor. To avoid the noise and clutter, Adam and the observer went to the basement, which was also cluttered with toys, but Adam "pushes the mess to one side."

After completing the questionnaire, the two returned upstairs, where "it seemed as though the adults live in one world, the kitchen, and the kids just run around everywhere else they want in their own little world." There were three women with their children at the house in addition to Ms. Banks and her children. Throughout the visit, Adam talked with a friend, played with the other children, and watched the television, occasionally "yelling" at another child to stop bothering him or "forcefully" moving them out of his way. When a baby cried, no adult would come to the baby; rather, the baby had to go to the kitchen to the adult. There was no discussion of school or schoolwork, and Adam did no homework or chores at all.

The scene was much the same when the observer arrived again: "Scattered toys, children running around." This time, Ms. Banks was the only adult present. Adam went to his bedroom, which was also full of scattered toys, but contained a television with a video game system that Adam began to play immediately. When a younger sister entered the room to crawl on Adam and the observer, he "kicks her out." She returned soon after with two other children, one of whom "starts throwing things" at the head of the observer. Adam then opened the door and screamed to his mother to get the children out of his room. Ms. Banks does not react, and another group of children enters the room.

A bit later, Ms. Banks calls Adam to sweep the kitchen, which he quickly does, before returning to his video game. The observer wrote in his notes, "I have no idea how [Adam] could develop good studying habits in this home. It seems as though there is always a constant flow of people going in and out, and on top of that, he has his brother, sisters, and cousins always bothering him." It is the responsibility of his mother to manage this household such that it is orderly, quiet, and structured enough for Adam to concentrate on his schoolwork, and that is clearly not being done, nor does Ms. Banks inquire about such work.

When Adam's friend takes out his cell phone, Adam "grabs at it and starts looking at it." Remember that these are ten- and eleven-year-old poor boys, one of whom has a cell phone. This is not the first time that we have seen very young poor students with cell phones, and I question the values and priorities of the adults who supply them. Adam and his friend then play games on the cell phone before returning to the video game. When the observer prepared to leave several hours later, he noted that there were now seven adults in the small house and "many children," a number of whom were in diapers.

Despite eight other attempts to meet with the family, the observer was not successful in observing the Banks family again. Although it is possible that the chaotic home environment changed, it is unlikely. Despite what both Adam and his mother replied to the questions from the questionnaire, there was absolutely no indication that education was at all important in this home. No attention was paid to anything related to school by Adam or by his mother, and even had Adam wanted to do homework, it was not possible in the environment in which he lives. Adam and the other children do mostly that which they want to do, when they want to do it, and this does not seem to include schoolwork. There was no discipline, no order, no real responsibility, no evidence of high educational aspirations, and no apparent effort to raise Adam's self-esteem. Indeed, none of the characteristics of the family life of high-achieving poor black students were present here, despite what Adam and Ms. Banks said.

LAUREL EBY

Laurel Eby is a ten-year-old fifth grader at one of the elementary schools attended by several other students, but not located near the neighborhood that is served by Family Focus. She is at grade level in all of her reading categories, each of the science categories, and the six social studies categories, but below grade level in two of the eight writing categories, and six of the ten math categories. I would classify her as a low-achieving student, though she is not far below. Her teacher indicates that she "still needs guidance in socially appropriate behavior," and that her father, who is the head of her household, needs to "continue to encourage" her to read after school and at home "at least thirty minutes a day." So, Laurel seems to have behavioral problems and needs help both with her reading and with her math.

Mr. Eby, who answered the questionnaire, grew up in Chicago, has lived in Evanston for four years, and is forty-nine years old. There are two children, including Laurel, in the home and Mr. Eby's twenty-two-year-old nephew "sticks around" the house. Mr. Eby works two full-time jobs, including one in the evening, which leaves him little time or energy for Laurel. Even if she wanted, for example, to participate in extracurricular activities, it would be difficult for Mr. Eby to support her, given that he would be at work. Mr. Eby is divorced and has a master's degree.

I have studied thirty-eight poor black and poor Latino families over the past four years, and only once before has the father in a family answered the questionnaire. In only one of the other poor black families observed has the father played any visible role in raising a child. Only twice before has a parent had a college degree. This makes the Eby family unique. This is a college-educated black man raising his children apparently by himself, but he works two full-time jobs to support the family.

Mr. Eby believes that his daughter's education is "extremely important, more important than anything" because "it's a catalyst for the future and for her to get a career. It's my job to have [Laurel] prepared for the outside world by the time that she turns eighteen." This is one of the very few cases in which the explanation for the importance of the education of the student did not focus exclusively upon getting a better job. Mr. Eby seems to look beyond the job market to understand the value of education. This is a characteristic of the middle class, no matter the income of a family. That is, middle-class families tend to understand better than others that education has value beyond jobs, and to therefore better prepare their children for that education, which in the case of public schools is essentially a middle-class enterprise. Poor families can indeed be middle class in their values, worldview, and approach to schools, and when they are, all other things being equal, their children do well in school. I have not seen this much in this research, and the grades of the children reflect this.

Mr. Eby says that he encourages Laurel to do well in school by asking about her homework and trying to be involved "when I can." I suspect that this involvement is limited by his work schedule. He visits her school often and feels "excited" when he does so. He wants Laurel "to excel," but points out that "she can get a little rowdy, but she has made great progress." He sees nothing getting in her way, and when asked whether any other student has tried to prevent Laurel from doing well in school, replied, "Not that she tells me." When asked whether race or discrimination played any role in his life, he responded, "Of course it does. In the schools there is always constitutional racism, there is that everywhere you go. There aren't as many opportunities available to [Laurel] as there are to some other kids. I wish it wasn't like that. Race plays a role in everything."

When asked about his upbringing, he mentioned that he grew up in Chicago in an "angry" and "very segregated" community with little exposure to "anything else." His father could pass for white and "we were beaten heavily" by his parents. "I don't hit my kids at all, nothing like what we got." He says that he only yells at them. In raising his children he is "nurturing," though he yells more than he should. He has "good talks" with Laurel; "we can talk out all of her problems." "We focus on education in our house." He reads the newspaper daily, unlike most of the adults interviewed, and notes that his job requires so much reading that he rarely reads anything else. Mr. Eby has had an addiction, and when he has a problem, he relies upon the program meant to deal with this and the people involved with the program. When asked whether there was anything else he wanted to add to the interview, he responded, "I want to know what my [Laurel] can do better, is there a way you can help me?" Obviously, this is a father who not only wants the best for his daughter but wants to know what to do to provide the best. He is even willing to ask for help. This in unheard of among the poor Latino and black men we have observed. These men, when present in the home, leave almost all of the child-rearing responsibilities to the mother, even when she works full time, which is the case among almost all of the black women observed.

Laurel indicated that she most likes her teacher "cause she helps me with my homework and she is really, really nice." She least likes "the people and how they is mean to me because they call me really mean names sometimes." She believes that she is doing well in school, and that her education is important "because if we don't get our education we'll be pretty stupid. Or if we don't have an education we won't ever get a job." According to Laurel, no other student has tried to prevent her from doing well in school, and she devotes "about three hours" to write papers or to do her math. It is not clear that she spends three hours a day on homework,

Laurel intends to go "all the way to college," and expects that her "dad will help" her to do so. When asked whether there are obstacles in her way, she replied that basketball and her friends were in her way. Apparently, Laurel believes that she devotes too much time to basketball and that her friends are obstacles for her. She says that she reads a newspaper once a week, and that her parents and family are the most important things in her life. She really feels close to her current teacher "because she really understands me a lot and is nice." When asked about race and discrimination, she indicated that she does not like Mexicans because the girl who is mean to her is Mexican, as is her mother. It is unclear whether she has a problem with Mexicans or with the other girl who happens to be Mexican. It is the case, however, that her feelings have apparently extended to include a group of people.

She says that she receives "a lot of help from mom and dad" with her schoolwork, and that they help her a lot, in fact, "too much." If she could change one thing about her life, it would be "to let my family be nicer to me." If she could be any one person in the world, she would be a model "because I want to walk the runway once." Laurel lives with her father, sister, and her adult cousin, who is described by Laurel as "a no good lazy who needed a job and free-loaded off of my dad." The cousin watched the television the entire time of the visit.

Laurel's bedroom is "a cramped room with a computer, desk, and bed." Above her door, she had written "This is [Laurel's] room so be quiet and let me get some peace and quiet." When the observer arrived, she was reading. The apartment is a three-bedroom apartment and each bedroom contained a computer. Laurel began her homework soon after the observer arrived. When she could not remember the assignment, she "walked around the house looking for her father." Once she remembered the assignment, her father showed her how to use e-library to help her to research her assignment. While she was at the computer, Mr. Eby watched over her shoulder. When her concentration waned, he held her in the chair and urged her to pay attention to her work. Laurel mentioned that she has a mentor who comes to her home three hours a week to help with her homework. While she seems to need extra help, which suggests that she is not doing very well in school, it appears that her father is prepared to arrange that help.

While Laurel completed her homework, her father made a jersey with a white t-shirt, which he painted because Laurel had forgotten her basketball jersey and needed it for a basketball game. While he did this,

Laurel "ran around the house," "tried to sneak in games to play on the computer," and "tried for her father not to catch her." She did not complete the homework before they rushed off to her basketball game. So, Laurel is involved with a basketball team, and her father seems dedicated to helping her as much as possible. He did, in fact, take the time to make her a basketball jersey because she had forgotten her jersey, and he did try to make certain that she did her homework and took her to her game.

This attention on his part must let Laurel know of his concern for her and her schoolwork. This is important for her self-esteem, for the value that she should give to her education, and for her sense of responsibility, all of which are very important to higher academic achievement. When the observer next met Laurel, she was at Family Focus "doing her homework," though she switched her "attention span between homework and other children." As I have indicated previously, Family Focus is not always the best place for students to do their homework, given that many of the children play rather do any homework, thereby becoming a distraction to other students. During the half hour at Family Focus, Laurel wrote a half a page, but she also played with other children. After the half hour, Laurel, her sister, and the observer left to go to the home of their babysitter who was not prepared for the observer and suggested that she should not go in because her house was "a mess."

According to Mr. Eby, when the girls leave school they are taken to Family Focus where (he believes) they do their homework and then go to the sitter's until he picks them up at 9 p.m., when he leaves his second job. As is the case for many of the poor students observed, Family Focus is a sort of babysitter until parents arrive home from work. In the case of the Eby family, however, since Mr. Eby works two jobs, there is another "babysitter" as well.

The next time the observer also met with Laurel at Family Focus. This time Laurel was not attempting to do homework. Rather, she was playing basketball, which she did until she and her sister left for the babysitter's house. When they arrived at the small one-story home, Laurel immediately turned the television on, though she did explain to the observer that she had a long list of homework to do. When the sitter came into the room to vacuum, Laurel turned up the volume on the television, but turned it down when the sitter told her to do so. The sitter asked whether she had any homework, to which Laurel replied, "Not really that I can do, just some papers for later." This was not exactly what she had told the observer.

We were only able to observe Laurel these three times, and only once in her home, so I am hesitant to draw any firm conclusions. However, the concern of Mr. Eby is not only evident but unusual for the black and Latino fathers observed over the years. He is not around enough, it seems to me, to do most of the things that need to be done if Laurel is to do well in school. Working two full-time jobs provides money but he cannot provide the time to consistently do that which he must do. Laurel arrives home late from the babysitter and, while she may then do her homework, it may also be that nine o'clock is late for her to begin this work. Poor single parents trying to provide for their children must balance work, raising their children, and preparing them for the school experience. It seems that the preparation often suffers in the process. Wanting to do the right things is not enough. Parents must know what to do and take the time to consistently do it. It is not clear that Mr. Eby knows or takes the time.

SUMMARY

Gutman and McLoyd (2000) found that the parents of poor black students who were high achievers helped them with their schoolwork "by tutoring them with practice sessions and problems" (10). On the other hand, the parents of low achievers "did not articulate using specific strategies to assist their children with their homework" (11). The parents of high achievers praised their children regularly for doing well, while the parents of low achievers did not. The parents of both high and low achievers indicate that education is very important for their children. In fact, Ms. Perez not only indicated this but cried out of frustration that her daughter, Alma, was doing poorly and she did not have any real idea of what to do to help. Mr. Eby wanted Laurel to do well, but he was not often at home to offer her help, even if he wanted to do so.

Among the characteristics of the homes of high-achieving poor black and Latino students are quiet, orderly, structured home environments.

It is difficult to do well with homework in a noisy, disruptive home environment in which it is not expected or required that homework be a top priority both for the parent and for the student. In the five households of the students I consider low achievers, these characteristics were, for the most part, missing. The television was often on, and other children often played and made noise while the student observed tried to do homework or to study, on the few occasions when they tried.

Aliyah Maxwell, Andre Hill, Adam Banks, and Laurel Eby seldom tried to do schoolwork, and no adult really made certain that they did so. The low-achieving students had no regularly assigned household chores, which help to teach responsibility and discipline. In fact, Aliyah Maxwell's mother told us that she tells her children to wash the dishes, but she generally ends up doing them herself.

While almost all of the five students considered to be low achievers indicated that they wanted to go to college, we heard no discussion of college during our observations. Indicating a desire to attend college in answer to a question from a questionnaire does not really suggest high educational aspirations. We heard no discussion among students or parents or between students or parents in these homes about college, despite the fact that the observers were all known to be college students and could therefore talk to parents and students about college. Laurel Eby's focus appears to be basketball, and Alma Perez is in danger of repeating second grade for a third time. In her case, however, her mother wants very badly for her to do better in school. She seems to have almost no idea of what to do to help her, and her inability to read or speak English is a very large problem for her. She not only cannot help Alma with her homework or reading but has difficulty understanding just what is going on at her school. This limits her involvement.

We observed virtually no attempts to discipline these five students, and no effort on the part of their parents to instill a sense of responsibility in them. Mr. Eby, a single black man raising his children alone, seems to want the best for Laurel, as is the case for almost all of the twenty-two parents or grandparents observed. However, he is not available to help her, even if he wanted to do so. The five parents say the right things in terms of the value of education and what they do to help their children, but they do very little in terms of the things needed to properly prepare the students for school. Whether this is because they do not know what to do, do not have the time to do it, or some other reasons, the fact remains that they fail to properly prepare their children for the educational experience.

I have indicated before (Sampson 2002) that the question of why some poor nonwhite parents do these things and others do not is beyond the scope of this research. We do see clearly, however, that when these things are done in the homes, the students tend to do well in school. When, as is the case with these five families, very few of the things are done, the students tend to do poorly. There will always be exceptions, and we assume that the proper things are in place in the schools. These five students are doing quite poorly in school, and their parents are not doing many of the things that they must do. Not race, poverty, or ethnicity explains this, for other poor black and Latino students are doing better, as we have seen.

7

DO SCHOOLS REALLY MATTER?

John Ogbu (2003) suggests that there are two sets of factors that affect minority students' performance: societal and school factors, and "community" factors, which include the beliefs and behaviors that "minority students bring to school" (xiii). It is my contention that, for the most part, these beliefs and behaviors are largely determined in the home. While this might suggest that research concerning the gap in academic performance between poor students and middle-income students, and between black and Latino students and Anglo students, focuses more on the home, this has not been the case. The overwhelming majority of the research on the educational achievement of poor nonwhites has focused upon school-related factors. Is this focus misguided?

As Gutman and McLoyd (2000, 3) correctly indicate, "Research on the family life of poor African-American children, however, is miniscule"—yet the home and the family are the key "ecological" settings for children. Much of the research on school achievement has focused upon school, in part because that research is easier to do, and because we believe that we can change schools. If we conclude that a school is failing to adequately educate children because it lacks sufficient funds, then we may be able to allocate more funds. If the school lacks adequately prepared or motivated teachers, then we may be able to change teachers. We can change administrators and alter the curriculum. We may be able to change the size of classes, though Howell and Peterson are not convinced that either money or class size makes that much difference in school performance (2002). We focus on schools because we can. In summarizing the research on effective schools, Howell and Peterson (2002) list as crucial factors: "a school's mission, its leadership, parental involvement, teacher expectations, and student homework" (102). We believe that we can alter the mission, change leadership, affect teacher expectations, change homework patterns, and that we can affect parental involvement.

The Chicago public schools require parents to pick up the report cards of students, thereby ensuring that parents will visit (become involved with?) the school several times a year. We try all sorts of things to increase parental involvement. The reality is, however, that the parents most likely to be involved with a school are most likely the parents who are already doing the things necessary to send their children to school prepared to learn—in other words, middle-class (not necessarily middle-income) parents. The parents who hold certain beliefs and attitudes and act upon them in certain ways in the home are more likely to both see the value of involvement and feel comfortable being involved. These are not, however, the parents who most *need* to be involved.

Parents who understand the need to raise the self-esteem of their children; who realize the value of a quiet, orderly home environment; who know just how important it is for them to not only check with their children concerning their homework but to work with them on it; who emphasize discipline, responsibility, and delayed gratification; who know that household chores and extracurricular activities contribute to both; and who stress high educational aspirations are parents who are more likely to become involved in the school. These are, however, the same parents who are more likely to have higher achieving students, because these characteristics are strongly correlated with achievement in public schools among poor nonwhite students (Clark 1983; Comer 1993; Bempechat 1998; Gutman and McLoyd 2000; Tapia 2000; Sampson 2002).

According to Irvine (1991), who cites Ianni (1987) and Walberg (1984), black parents who talk to their children every day about their schoolwork and what they learned, read to their children, take them to the library, supervise their homework, encourage them, and monitor the watching of television "significantly increase their children's academic learning" (110). Ogbu (2003), too, notes the negative impact of television watching on the academic performance of black students. In this research, I found that most of the low-achieving poor black and poor Latino students, and many of the average students, watched the television every day after school, often while attempting to do their homework. The needed parental supervision was lacking.

In fact, I found that the parents of the below-average students and some of the average students rarely talked to their children about school, and then only in very general terms. This is not a part of the prescription for academic success offered by Irvine (1991) for black students. Irvine, while acknowledging that all black students are not the same, nevertheless goes on to treat them as though they are in her work, though she does point out social class differences. I believe that the social class issue is misunderstood all too often. Class is more about beliefs, attitudes, and behavior than it is about education, occupation, and income.

Poor folks can and do have some of the beliefs, attitudes, values, and behavior that we think characterize the middle class. If they did not, almost none would get out of poverty. Given that public schools are, as Comer (1993) tells us, middle-class institutions, it should not surprise us that those poor nonwhite students who are raised in a home environment that we have generally assumed was the exclusive province of the middle-income folks, manage, all other things being equal, to do well in school. Poor nonwhite families may all be poor and all nonwhite, but they are not all "lower class." Some have the discipline, sense of responsibility, ability to delay gratification, internal control, "frustration tolerance" (Comer 1993), and high expectations that we generally associate with the middle class.

If, however, poor students go to school with teachers who immediately categorize and stigmatize them as low achievers lacking high educational expectations, then they are unlikely to teach them or to challenge them. If they attend schools in which the administrators fail to pay attention to the actions of teachers and to correct them, then teachers are unlikely to properly serve the students. If the facilities are inadequate, then the performance may well suffer. Because of these considerations, I do not suggest that schools are not important in addressing the academic success of poor nonwhites.

However, since *A Nation at Risk* (National Commission 1983) was released, our focus has been upon changing schools, and there is little evidence to suggest that the changes have had a significant impact upon the performance of poor black or poor Latino students. There have been small successes here and there but, for the most part, poor black and poor Latino students are no better off today than thirty years ago. We have changed curricula, changed control of schools, looked for better-trained teachers and administrators, tried smaller schools and longer school years, and we are trying vouchers and charter schools. On the margins, some of these changes have had a positive impact. For the most part, however, poor black and poor Latino students are still far behind the nonpoor and white students (Irvine 1991; Valdes 1998; Ogbu 2003).

I am not suggesting that we ignore school changes. I am suggesting that we begin to focus on home changes, and I do not mean by this the superficial issue of parental involvement in school-related activities, which will often alienate many poor parents because the schools are middle-class institutions. The middle-class poor parents may well be able to deal with this type of involvement, though it is not easy for some of them. Teachers are well-educated, well-spoken, well-dressed people. Many poor people are none of these, and many poor Latinos do not even speak the English being spoken by most teachers, coaches, and administrators, let alone the educational jargon.

In fact, for the most part, the Latino parents observed for this research not only could not speak English but consequently could not help their children with their homework or really discuss with them school-related activities. These are two of the most important things parents can do to help with performance. After observing poor Latino families for some two years, Tapia (2000) concludes that the academic achievement of Mexican Americans can best be understood through the analysis of the household and by observing the school-related activities of family members, not by looking to schools or classrooms. Schools are important, but families are crucial if we want to improve the academic performance of poor black and poor Latino students.

BLACKS AND LATINOS

The most obvious difference between the poor black and poor Latino families studied in this research is the language difference. In three of the five Latino households observed, the parent interviewed spoke little or no English—yet the schoolwork and information from school were generally in English, making it very difficult for the parent to interact with the student in terms of schoolwork. I have the impression that these parents wanted very badly, for the most part, for their children to do well in school. In fact, they often asked the observer to serve as a tutor for their children. In the homes in which the parents spoke only Spanish, the observer spoke Spanish as well.

On a number of occasions, the parent asked the observer to tell them what they could do to help their child to do better in school. We also observed what some refer to as a gender difference in the raising of the Latino children, which may well have an impact upon their academic achievement. Valdes (1998) writes, "Boys are raised by their mothers and fathers to be 'macho' or manly. Girls are raised to be 'mujeres buenas' or decent women" (14). The boys are supposed to be protectors and defenders, and the girls to be virgins at marriage; the boys to make money to support their family, and the girls to grow up and have a family; the boys to be aggressive, and the girls passive and reticent. If the boys are groomed to take care of their families, to make a living as soon as possible, then they may well have little need for education. After all, they can find some job at a fairly young age and help to care for their immediate family.

Several of the young boys we observed seemed to do as they pleased, which often did not include anything related to school. If the top priority for young Latinas is to be good girls and raise a family, of what value is education? The Latino students whom we observed were almost never involved in extracurricular activities. If the forms required for these school-based activities are sent home in English, the parents would have a difficult time with them. Further, it is not clear that the parents understood the value of such activities. Although a number of the black students were involved in these activities, for the most part, the black students observed were not as involved as would be expected for high achievers. It seems that neither the Latino parents nor most of the black parents placed any importance upon this involvement, and neither did their children.

Few of the black parents participated in what Irvine refers to as the "curriculum of the home" (1991, 110). That is, few were involved on a daily basis with the school lives of the students in their homes. This was

also the case for the Latino parents, though several of them indicated a
desire to be so involved. All the black parents indicated that education
was important to them and said that they helped their child to do well
in school. This was simply not the case in reality, at least not on a consistent basis; they said one thing and did another. This was also true for
the Latino parents, but several of them also said that they wished that
they knew what to do to help; only one black parent said this.

A male was in the homes of all of the Latino families observed, which
was true for only a few of the black families observed. With the exception of the two black women who were unemployed and the one who
was ill, all of the black women observed worked outside of the home and
had no visible support from a man in dealing with the children. This, of
course, has not only economic implications but also means that they
have less time and energy to do the kinds of things needed to properly
prepare their children for school. While the Latino families had a male
present, we did not see any of them play an active role in the preparation of the children for school. The males were, by and large, not present in the homes of the poor black families observed, and though present in the poor Latino families, played no visible role in the school
preparation. This places an enormous burden upon the women in the
homes of the black and Latino families, but since almost all of the black
women work outside of the home, while most of the Latinas do not, that
burden may be greater for the black women.

Part of this burden might be the lack of time to support the child's
participation in extracurricular activities, which generally take place after school, or to visit the student's school during the school day. We saw
little evidence of such support and very little of these visits during our
observations of either black or Latino families. Then, too, Grossman
(1995) suggests that Latinos tend to be very respectful of authority,
which would include teachers and administrators. This may lead to a
failure of Latinos to question teachers or administrators. We heard very
little criticism or questioning of school personnel or activities from the
Latino parents; occasionally a black parent had some criticism of the
school. For the most part, however, we did not observe a great deal of
involvement in school-related activities on the part of either the Latino
or the black parents, and, of course, we observed only three students
whose academic performance I would consider above average.

For the most part, the poor black and poor Latino families were much the same in terms of the way in which they approached school preparation. The two big differences on the part of the Latina mothers have to do with language and expressed interest in learning what needs to be done in order for their children to perform better. The Latino families may also allow the boys more latitude than is the case for the black families, but a number of the black male students showed little discipline, sense of responsibility, ability to delay gratification, or internal control. I am not certain that they differ that much in terms of the expectations of males as opposed to females.

A CULTURE OF LOW EXPECTATIONS

Some scholars, such as Irvine (1991) and Boykin (1986), have argued that blacks do not do as well in school as whites because of cultural differences between the blacks who attend the schools and the whites who teach, develop the curriculum, and administer the schools. I believe that this argument is overly simplistic in that it ignores the differences among blacks. Upper-income blacks are not the same as those on welfare, and middle-income urban blacks are certainly not the same as poor rural blacks. They have little in common beyond race. Ogbu (2003) examined the cultural conflict argument and found little empirical support for it in his latest work. He did not find the differences in movement, time orientation, or verve that Boykin (1986) found to limit the academic success of black students. Although I did not address these variables in this study, I did find that, for the most part, poor black students are doing fairly well in a largely white, middle-income environment, and those who are doing fairly well have a number of the same family characteristics.

I am less concerned with a black culture that limits academic achievement than with a culture of low academic expectations. As I have indicated, almost all of the parents interviewed indicated that they value the education of their child, encourage their child to do well, and believe that little stands in the child's way in terms of receiving a good education. However, few of them do most of the things at home that will help the child to do well in school. They say one thing and do another at home.

In a poor black community in which the most successful people may appear to be the drug sellers, and in which few people have attended college, it may be difficult to stimulate the young people toward education. Of what value is it? After all, who besides the teachers do they see every day who has benefited from it? Then, too, the society expects poor black students to perform poorly in school, so many students have this built-in excuse for failure. Not much is expected of them, so not much needs to be put out. Still, a host of the poor black students in such communities do well in school. This is a testament to the work of their parents and perhaps those in the school they attend.

Ogbu (2003) points out that the black students in his study were characterized by "low effort syndrome." That is, they did not work very hard on their schoolwork, and they acknowledged this failure to work hard. Although Ogbu studied middle-income blacks, I observed poor blacks, and I believe that this lack of effort goes beyond what he refers to as "academic disengagement" for many poor blacks. Rather, it is part of a culture of low expectations. Poor black students understand fairly early that the role models that they see in their communities did not benefit from doing well in school and begin to question why they should do well. They do not see a huge price to pay for doing poorly. Their parents want them to do better than they did but, for the most part, that is not asking for very much, and college, for example, is not required for this.

Many of their teachers understand that the student may well not escape the ghetto, that the parent is not doing many of the right kinds of things at home, and that the student is not working hard on schoolwork. Why should they work hard? The black students in Shaker Heights, the site of Ogbu's work, see middle-income, successful blacks every day who have benefited from education. High expectations on their part and on the part of their parents and school personnel make sense. The culture of the black ghetto, which I contend has more to do with generations of poverty than with race, does not expect or require much of the students or of their parents. Still, a number of the parents we observed struggle to do what they believe are the right things for their children.

How does a parent inspire a student to aim for college, and to therefore work hard in school to get there, when no one in the family has attended college, when high school graduation was a stretch for many in the family? Although this happens, and we saw it happen, it is not easy to do. Irvine (1991), in referring to the work of Weis (1985), pointed out that black students wanted to go to college and to escape poverty but were negligent in their schoolwork. She goes on the mention the work of Howard and Hammond (1986), which attributes the lack of achievement on the part of blacks to the acceptance on their part of the view of society that they are not likely to succeed. She sees this as a part of black culture. I see this as a part of the culture of low expectations. There is nothing "black" about it. The urban poor are disproportionately black, and little is expected of them. Many, therefore, give little. A number, however, give more and achieve more, as we have seen in this work.

The situation may be different for many of the poor Latinos. Grossman (1995) argues that many Latinos do indeed face a cultural conflict that may impede academic success. He mentions a tendency on the part of Latinos toward cooperation, consensus building, and working in groups, which conflicts with the emphasis in American education upon competition and individual achievement. Although it is not clear just how long these cultural characteristics last as Latinos become Americanized, it is true that most of the parents we observed still speak Spanish in the home, and read and write little English. This might indicate that significant cultural differences still survive on the part of the parents. The children, though, may be torn between the American culture stressed in the schools and the Latino culture alive in the home. If this is the case, it would be difficult for the parents to help to prepare the children, given the difference in their orientation and the one stressed in school.

Tapia (2000), while mentioning Mexican American culture, stresses the importance of the home and community conditions as influences of academic achievement among poor Mexican Americans. He does not stress cultural differences, and I did not see much evidence of those differences, with the possible exception of the gender difference. Consistent with my notion of a culture of low expectations, he writes, "These incidents reflect how the academic development of successful students can be sidetracked by the lack of enough people in their environment with high levels of education that are more characteristic of middle-class neighborhoods" (36). While I believe that he misuses the term *middle-class*, his point is well taken. Successful black and Latino people who have used education to become successful are rather rare in the barrio or the ghetto. Integration has allowed and encouraged them to move out of predominately Latino or black neighborhoods, taking with them their value as role models, the stability they provided, and their impact upon the schools.

Their presence does not guarantee academic success, as Ogbu (2003) shows us. Remember, however, that the middle-income black students studied by Ogbu performed better than blacks, not only in Ohio but throughout America. They were not doing as well as whites or as well as their parents wanted them to do, however. Ogbu did not study the family lives of these students.

Clearly, families have an enormous impact upon the academic success of students, an impact I believe to be greater than that of the schools, all other things being equal. Poor black and poor Latino families may well have to deal with gangs, drugs, financial difficulties, working parents, and school personnel who know little about these difficulties. Yet a number of them still manage to do a number of the things needed of them in order for their children to do well in school. We did not observe many of them engaged in activities designed to raise the self-esteem of their children. Nor did we see many encourage their children to participate in extracurricular activities or to do household chores. Many failed to provide a quiet, orderly, structured home environment, or to work on the ability to delay gratification in their children. A number did not stress discipline. However, some did stress discipline and responsibility, and some did make certain that the television was off. Some did ask about the school day and homework, and some tried to help with the work, though in a few cases language was a problem. Some encouraged the extracurricular activities. So some parents, despite the obstacles, tried to do some of the things that help students to do well in school, and others did not, and the grades of many of the students seem to reflect the differences.

8

SO WHAT DOES IT MEAN?

Julia Wrigley, in her foreword to Lareau's book (2000), writes, "Teacher quality is the single most important school factor affecting children's learning" (x). She goes on to point out that class size also has an impact upon students in elementary schools, and to note that "parental savvy" has become a salient part of the discussion of improving student performance, and therefore, I would add, in the discussion of educational policy, which has an impact upon that performance. The problem is that, for the most part, the discussion of educational policy has centered on such variables as teacher quality, class size (and therefore funding), school governance, and parental involvement in the schools themselves.

A small but growing body of research suggests that, at a minimum, we shift some of our attention to changes in this policy in order to stress the role of the parents in the preparation of their children for the school experience. Jean Murphy (2003), in writing about the four young black students she studied (though she does not tell us just how she studied these four students), notes, "All four benefit from the continuous, active involvement of their parents in guiding and influencing their school success. Their families pass on cultural values and use intentional behaviors that support and advance academic success" (85). While I have some problems with her idea that some of these behaviors and values are "cultural" in a racial sense, I believe that the data clearly suggest not only that what parents do at home influences how well students do in school but also in pointing out precisely what it is that parents need to do.

The studies that follow families in depth to ascertain what they do in their homes to influence the performance of the students in the schools tend to be small in scope because of the nature of the research. It is therefore important for scholars to engage in more of this research in order for us to build a base and to increase our confidence in the findings. Tapia (2000) observed four Mexican American households. Murphy (2003) observed four black households. Clark (1983) studied ten poor black households. Lareau studied twelve white families. For this work, I observed seventeen poor black and Latino families. I have, however, observed twelve poor black households for a previous study (Sampson 2002) and nine poor Latino families for an earlier work (Sampson 2003). The body of work that focuses upon the role of the family is growing, as is our confidence in the findings.

I am not suggesting that we ignore factors other than family-related behaviors in our discussion of changes in educational policy that might improve the academic performance of poor blacks and Latinos. Some school-related variables must be addressed, and all other things need to be equal for the family variables to have maximum effect. For many poor students, all other things are seldom equal, and they must be addressed. Plus, peers may affect performance (Ogbu 2003; Goodenow and Grady 1994) as well. This equation is not a simple one. However, we are learning just what poor black and poor Latino families do in the home that is associated with the higher academic performance of their children, and it may well be time that what we are learning be included in the discussion of public policy changes designed to improve the education offered to poor nonwhites. As Lareau shows us, parental behavior is key to the performance of the nonpoor and poor alike, regardless of race. However, given the dismal performance of blacks, Latinos, and of the poor overall, and the gap in the performance between poor blacks and poor Latinos with the nonpoor and whites, I believe that we need to focus upon poor blacks and Latinos.

Educational policy needs to begin with the understanding that not all poor Latinos and poor black students do poorly in school, and needs to be crafted to deal with those who do poorly and to support those who do well. The findings suggest to me that we begin to think seriously about a family intervention policy that identifies the family characteristics of low-achieving poor black and Latino students, develops individual curricula for each family centered on what we know to be the characteristics of the families of high and perhaps average achievers, and then teach the families what they need to do and how to do it.

Schools cannot do this, though they can and should help. For one thing, the task will require more time and energy than most school personnel have after doing their jobs. For another, schools and school personnel often intimidate poor nonwhite parents, given their middle-class orientation and style. Finally, those folks who can go into the homes of the poor, convince them that they need change, and gain their confidence to allow this process of change to proceed will have to have earned the trust of the parents. These folks are more likely to be community-based outreach workers than school personnel. These workers can be trained based upon the findings of myself and others to understand that student and parental behavior is associated with higher academic performance. They must, however, take into consideration that many poor families face daily obstacles and problems that they believe take precedence over the school performance of their children. Rent must be scraped together. Money for food is not always available. Illness may be catastrophic, given the lack of health insurance. Drugs, as we have seen, may be an issue.

These and other survival issues take their toll on a number of poor folks, particularly poor Latinos and blacks. Others may not see the value of the work that they must do, given that education may well not have helped folks they know to climb out of the barrio or the ghetto. Many parents, however, want to know what they need to do differently or better, despite these other problems; based upon what we have seen and heard, I believe that this is particularly the case among many poor Latinos. We can reach some of these parents, and we can improve the academic performance of many of their children. This requires the collaboration of community-based agencies, schools, and perhaps the scholars who know what goes on in the homes of those who do well in school.

Schools can inform the agencies about who does well and who does not. Once an intervention plan is in place, teachers should be aware of this and be especially attuned to the need to boost the self-esteem of those students involved in the program, given that they may be under increased stress because they will be the focus of a fairly long-term effort, and that they will have nonfamily members in their homes for some time. Although not all of the training needs to take place in homes, and some may take place in groups, a community-based worker will need to be in homes over time. Teaching a parent what delayed gratification means and its value is important. Ensuring that the parent says and does what needs to be done and said daily to teach the student to delay gratification takes time and consistency.

Ogbu (2003) briefly examines a number of school-based policy approaches designed to improve the performance of black students. He writes, "Common to these approaches is an assumption that conventional public school policy and practices are the reasons why Black students are not academically successful" (265). He rejects this assumption and goes on to argue, "To date there is no convincing evidence that these strategies are more effective than conventional public school practices in increasing the academic achievement of Black students" (267). He looks at school choice, vouchers, charter schools, performance contracts, and merit pay for teachers based upon their performance. Each of these approaches is to one degree or another a market-driven approach, and Ogbu does not believe that they will have much impact on improving the education of black students. He also questions what he refers to as "culturally responsive education." I agree with Ogbu on both counts.

There is little to suggest that the latest policy change options will significantly improve the education of black students generally, and poor black students specifically. Nor do I think that they will help many poor Latinos. Ogbu studied a different economic group of blacks than did I, and had a somewhat different research focus. As a result, his policy recommendations are different. However, one of those recommendations is that black parents "should be involved in their children's education at home. We are, therefore, recommending parent education on how to promote their children's school success at home. The community, not the school district, should take the initiative in providing this education for parents. The community should develop both for-profit and not-for-profit programs to teach parents how to help their children with academic and nonacademic school problems" (280).

Despite the fact that we have studied very different populations in very different ways, and for different reasons, we still come to the same conclusion in terms of policy change, and Ogbu wants this intervention for middle-income black parents whose children perform better than other black students in their state and in the country. I want the changes for poor black and poor Latino students who are performing worse than other poor black and poor Latino students. Because Ogbu studied the schools and the community of blacks in Shaker Heights, Ohio, he is in position to recommend policy efforts by the schools and the community. My focus has been families, and I am therefore limited to recommendations regarding families.

Ogbu (2003) did recommend a number of themes on which the Minority Achievement Committee in Shaker Heights might focus, which are very close to a number of the characteristics that I and others have found in the homes of the higher achievers, including role models, a future orientation, responsibility, and discipline. I believe that these are among the characteristics that must be instilled into those poor blacks and poor Latinos who want to see their children improve and are willing to do the things required for this to happen. Some poor black and Latino parents have issues such as drugs or alcohol or severe financial difficulties or emotional problems that must be addressed, probably before they can even begin to think about improvements in their home lives that will enhance the academic performance of their children. As Clark (1983, 211) put it, "But, practically speaking, parents in these communities are in dire need of well-conceptualized or support efforts to offset or 'buffer' the tremendous psychic overload they routinely experience." Others may not care much about this performance. We cannot reach every family. We can, however, reach some, and for the most part, except for some small-scale community-generated efforts around the nation, we are currently reaching almost none of the families most in need.

Thought must also be given to the role of language in the poor Latino households. Sanchez (1997) suggests that using Spanish to begin the instruction of Latino students has advantages, but also has the disadvantage of segregating those students within the school, which is a serious disadvantage. He suggests, therefore, using Spanish to begin the child's education on a partial basis in schools, though he also notes the problems with this approach. Given that almost all of the scholars who have studied the role of the family in the education of poor nonwhites point to the importance of the involvement of a parent in the schoolwork of the student, and that many poor Latino parents cannot really play this role because the student's schoolwork comes home in English, these parents simply cannot do that which is perhaps most important for the child.

If the work comes home in Spanish, the parents can do that which helps the child, but this requires more bilingual teachers and probably some degree of segregation of the child within the schools. Furthermore, much of the basic communication between schools and homes is in English. This means that many Latino parents cannot even understand what is going on in the schools or perhaps with their children. For a different study, we observed two poor Latino families in which a letter informing the parents that the student was being held back a grade in one family and a report card indicating that the child was well below grade level in about everything were discarded by the students after they informed their mothers that they were doing well in school. The mothers simply could not understand what the communications meant. This may also limit the participation of the child in extracurricular activities. At the beginning, at least, any efforts to train poor Latino parents must therefore be made in Spanish for those families in which only Spanish is spoken by the parents.

This alone is not enough, however, if parents cannot read or understand the communications from the school to them. Some consideration should be given to a solution to this problem in communities in which school–home communications are only in English. The price to pay for success in American society has long been assimilation. That is, we require groups to blend in, to give up that which makes them different in order for them to function well in this society. Some might suggest, by the way, that even that price has not been enough for blacks as a group. Latinos may maintain their cultural differences; again, Latinos are not all the same, in part through the language difference. If we ask them to give up this difference, we may well be asking them to give up their cultural differences, which they may not want to do. We need to approach this issue carefully and in a sensitive manner.

I do not take a position on the delicate and contentious issue of whether the poor Latinos I have studied should have to learn English. I believe that they want to be better parents, for the most part, and that we are beginning to learn precisely what they need to do in order for that to happen. We should now begin to reach out to them with programs of change to allow this. The community-based organizations that must teach them what they need to know will typically know how to handle the language issue, but it must be addressed, and schools may well have to be involved in the effort.

People in this society, including most scholars who study education and race/ethnicity, seem to believe that blacks and Latinos generally, and poor blacks and poor Latinos in particular, do poorly in school. In reality, while they generally do worse than middle-income students and white students (who are quite often middle income), many do reasonably well in school. Our generalizations are flawed, and perhaps dangerously so. Yes, there is a gap in performance between blacks and whites (Whittington 1996) and between Anglos and Latinos (Darder, Torres, and Gutierrez 1992). However, some black and some Latino families, even poor families, do some of the things necessary in the home in order for their children to perform well in school, and some do most of the things required. As a result, their children, despite great obstacles, do quite well in school.

The task ahead is to shift some of the focus from schools to families. Some poor black and poor Latino families are for educational purposes middle-class families in terms of their beliefs, attitudes, and behavior in the home. I cannot determine why some families are middle class and poor and therefore properly prepare their children for school, while some of those living in the same neighborhood, with students in the same schools, and at the same income level are not. This issue is beyond my data, though it is a very interesting issue. Clark (1983) also found that some poor black families did the right things, while others did not, and attributed the difference to "deep emotional turmoil [that] abounded due to long-term powerlessness, mistrust, discord, confusion, and anger" (210). He still did not explain why these characteristics existed for some poor blacks and not for some of their neighbors.

I did not detect much anger or mistrust on the part of many of the poor blacks or poor Latino parents we observed, even among those whose children were doing very poorly. Parents who are overwhelmed by stress and obligation may have little time or energy to play the role of teacher at home, and we did not attempt to measure the level of stress, confusion, or obligation. But we do know that some parents in apparently very similar circumstances can and do play the role quite well. This suggests that others can be trained to do so as well. This training may need to consider gender differences in performance, given that all three of the above-average students observed are girls. There were, on the other hand, several girls among the below-average achievers. While I am not as convinced of the difference as are Gutman and McLoyd (2000), it may bear further scrutiny. Neither Ogbu (2003), Clark (1983), nor Tapia (2000) made mention of such differences, but future researchers may want to consider them.

EPILOGUE: A RETURN
TO THE BEGINNING

Four years ago, we observed twelve poor black students within the context of their families in order to examine the role of the family in the academic achievement of poor black students. (Sampson 2002). The families all lived in the poor west-side neighborhood in Evanston in which Family Focus is located, and six of the twelve students attended the same middle school attended by the majority of students in that neighborhood. I classified six of the twelve students as high achievers, three as average students, and three as low achievers. Recently, we observed five of the original twelve families again in order to ascertain the extent to which the impact of the family preparation for school lasts in terms of grades, and to develop greater confidence in our findings.

I wanted to see whether the achievement levels of students changed over the four years and to learn what changes in preparation were in place four years later. I had intentionally focused on students in the middle-school age group both because they receive letter grades in Evanston, which allows easier comparisons of achievement levels, and because the preparation of the student by the family is likely to be very different for older students, and we wanted a better understanding of the differences, if any, in this preparation. While I have focused primarily upon middle school and upper-level elementary school students in this work, believing that preparation patterns need to be in place sooner rather than later for students, and that those patterns may well be different for older students who have already been prepared, both Clark (1983) and Ogbu (2003) have studied high school students. I still believe that if changes in the family preparation are to take place, they are better made sooner. The observations of the five families four years later allows us the opportunity to determine whether these preparation strategies change over time, and how successful they were over time in terms of achievement.

STEPHANIE ADAMS

Stephanie Adams was a thirteen-year-old seventh grader living with both parents and four siblings. During the second grading period, she received two grades of B+, one B, two B- grades, and one C. While these grades were down slightly from the first grading period, she clearly was a high achiever. When her mother, Ms. Adams, was asked how important Stephanie's education was to her, Ms. Adams replied, "It's really important. No one is complete without education." This answer stands in stark contrast to the answers to that question given by most of the parents observed for this study. Remember that in most cases these parents indicated that the education of their child was important, but the reason given related in most instances to the job market and not to some "higher" goal. Ms. Adams seemed to look beyond the job market for Stephanie, suggesting a broader worldview.

When asked about her upbringing, Ms. Adams indicated that she was raised in a disciplined and structured home, which gave a hint about how Stephanie was raised. She also told us that she helped Stephanie with her homework, and that she "provides every possible support she needs" in order for Stephanie to do well in school. Many parents have told us much the same thing, only for us to observe something very different. In the case of the Adams family, however, what we were told was precisely that which we observed. Four years later, Stephanie's education was still very important to Ms. Adams because "Without an education you will get lost or be cheated. You need to have education to survive." She still appears to be looking beyond the job market.

Ms. Adams told us that she attends Stephanie's school for parent-teacher conferences, and for sports and awards banquets. Stephanie was involved in several extracurricular activities, including sports, four years ago, and was apparently still involved in them. Ms. Adams said that if anything stood in her daughter's way in terms of her receiving a good education, she "would get it off her at any cost," which hints at the dedication she has to her role in the education of her daughter. Four years ago, Ms. Adams did not believe that other students tried to prevent Stephanie from doing well in school. Now, however, she believes that other students try to pressure her to perform less well. Stephanie has performed very well for at least four years, and it may well be that others realize that she is an outstanding student over time, which may to some degree take away their excuse for failure. This is, after all, a relatively poor black student who has been an outstanding student both in and out of the classroom for some time, suggesting that achievement is possible and sustainable for poor blacks. This makes some look bad, and they may attempt to pressure Stephanie in order to avoid this.

Ms. Adams told us this time that she teaches Stephanie how to discipline herself, and that "education is key to life." She still stresses discipline. Stephanie was a sixteen-year-old tenth grader when we observed her for this research. Her cumulative grade point average was a 3.5, and her average was 3.6 for the last grading period. She had three A- grades, two B+ grades, and a C grade. Stephanie is still an outstanding student four years later. When we asked her four years ago why her education was very important to her, she replied, "It impacts my future," suggesting a future orientation that goes beyond a decent job. She indicated that she studied one to two hours a day and that she wanted to go to law school. This time she told us that her education was important because "education is the key to success and to life," so she is still looking to the future.

Both times, she told us that other students have tried to prevent her from doing well in school. This time she said that it happens "often" and that friends want her to "hang out" while she knows that she has work to do. They do not want her to be a "bookworm." Stephanie now wants to achieve a PhD and expects to do so. This is a tenth grader who expects to receive a PhD! Many university students have no clue about their future and virtually no expectations. Stephanie now tells us that she studies every evening for seven to eight hours a night. This is a big increase from the seventh-grade years, but the workload has no doubt increased as well. She apparently has adjusted to the load.

Stephanie indicated that her parents help her with her schoolwork "whenever I ask for it. They also ask me about my progress if I don't ask them. They are concerned." This is precisely what parents should do on a consistent basis if they want their children to be successful in school. They must monitor the schoolwork and progress all of the time, an act that shows the student not only how important the work really is but also shows the student how important she is, thus supporting higher self-esteem.

The dominant themes in the Adams home four years ago were discipline, responsibility, structure, order, delayed gratification, schoolwork, extracurricular activities, and parental supervision of and involvement in Stephanie's activities, all characteristics of the homes of high achievers. In some ways, it was the model high-achieving home. During the first observation four years ago when Ms. Adams arrived home from work, she discussed the day's events with her children, including Stephanie's injury during her soccer practice. Ms. Adams immediately asked a younger son whether he had completed his homework and said his prayers. When he replied that he had not yet said the prayers, she told him "Now." She asked another son who had made dinner that night, suggesting that the children have household responsibilities.

Ms. Adams constantly praised her children, but also constantly made certain that they did their chores and their homework. Stephanie was still doing her homework an hour after she began and the observer left. During another observation at their Islamic worship center, Stephanie took charge of a group of younger children, demonstrating leadership ability and high self-esteem. During another observation, one of the boys cooked dinner while Stephanie worked on her homework. When Ms. Adams arrived from work, she asked her children about their chores and whether they had prayed. Stephanie worked on her homework for some two hours. On another evening, Ms. Adams was observed discussing school grades with Stephanie before asking whether she had completed her homework. Stephanie also informed the observer that she participated in both soccer and track. The pattern was about the same every evening: the children worked on homework, or in the case of the younger boys, watched the television; did their household chores;

and when their mother arrived from work, discussed their days with her and answered her questions about their days and the chores.

Each evening Stephanie did her chores and her homework after practice, often devoting hours to the homework. If the chores were not completed, Ms. Adams let the "offenders" know that she was not happy. She was a loving, caring mother who stressed discipline, responsibility, and schoolwork, and who was in constant touch with her children even though she arrived from work late in the evening.

When the observer arrived for the first visit four years later, Stephanie had yet to arrive from school at 6:30 p.m. When she did arrive, she immediately began to do her household chores, while one of her younger brothers told the observer that he had been with a friend when the friend broke a window. Wanting to avoid being blamed, the Adams boy ran away. Ms. Adams admonished him for failing to approach the owner of the window to tell him the identity of the guilty party. Ms. Adams is still stressing a sense of responsibility for her children. Throughout the evening, Stephanie worked on her homework, as she had done years earlier.

During the next visit, Ms. Adams was "elated" at the opportunity to discuss with the observer Stephanie's participation in the state championship track meet. Her school had, in fact, won the championship, and Stephanie had run three events for her school. Ms. Adams had attended the meet, which took place out of town. So Stephanie was still involved in extracurricular activities, her mother still supported her, and Stephanie still centers her evenings on her chores and her homework. When Stephanie arrived, Ms. Adams immediately questioned her about some make-up work she had to do. When told that Stephanie had not yet completed the work, Ms. Adams "demeanor changed at this point," as she let Stephanie know that she was not happy about this. Stephanie did the dishes and told the observer that she hoped that college would be easier because she was under great stress at this point. She told the observer that college was not an option in her house, it was "inevitable"; she had no choice but to attend college. The expectations of her family are still high, but Stephanie indicated that she was comfortable with this because it showed that her parents were concerned about her.

When Ms. Adams arrived home from work at the time of the next visit, she "made sure that the children had completed their homework and that they had started their chores," something she did every night and had done every time we were in the home both four years ago and recently. Stephanie arrived late as usual, and her parents reminded her that she often had the observer waiting for her, which was not acceptable. She explained that she was a bit late because she had to complete the make-up work and to see a physics tutor. They accepted this explanation, but the fact that they wanted her to be on time suggests, again, their emphasis upon responsibility and discipline. She then showed her parents her homework and progress reports. Ms. Adams was happy that she was doing better in two of her classes, and told Stephanie that she was pleased that she would not now have to stop competing in track due to her grades. Stephanie is an outstanding student, but if she was not doing as well as her parents expected, she would be forced by them to limit her extracurricular activities. They expect high performance and are not afraid to take action if they do not see it.

Little has changed in the Adams household. Ms. Adams still routinely oversees the children's performance of their chores and the completion of their homework. Stephanie is still an outstanding student, now at one of the nation's best high schools, is still very responsible and very disciplined. Ms. Adams is still involved with the school-related activities of her children, and still makes a point of supporting their high self-esteem. The house is still orderly, quiet, and structured, and almost everything is centered on education and responsibility. Ms. Adams does about everything a parent of a high-achieving student should do and has been observed doing. She has done these things now for at least four years, and the pattern has changed very little, even though Stephanie is now a sophomore in high school. This suggests both that we can have more confidence in our findings given the consistency over time, and that good students will remain good students if their family environment remains supportive.

TRACEY LOVE

Tracey was an eleven-year-old sixth grader and an average student when we last observed her. She attended a different school than that attended by most of the students from her neighborhood, but which was attended by two other students from the original study. She received three C+ grades, one C-, one B-, and one B+ in the latest grading period four years ago. Her mother, Ms. Love, believed four years ago that Tracey's education was very important because it helped her with self-awareness, and because education would provide "a more secure future." She said that she helped and encouraged Tracey by asking about her homework and asking about her goals in education. She believed that there was some peer pressure on Tracey to perform poorly, and she was raised in a very religious environment in which education was not stressed.

She tries to raise Tracey with an emphasis upon values, being the best that she can be, education, and religion. Her education was important to Tracey because "I want to be smart, get a good education while in college, and one day have a family." She told us that while in the fifth grade a peer tried to convince her to skip class "because she didn't study so therefore she didn't want me to do well." This supports Ogbu's (2003) thesis concerning pressure on some black students by others to perform poorly to justify their own poor performance, a thesis for which I have not seen a great deal of support but which, nevertheless, makes a great deal of sense.

Tracey told us four years ago that she devoted two and a half hours a day to her homework and that she expects to go to graduate school. Like Stephanie, if she could be any one person in the world, she would be herself. Both young ladies appeared to have more self-confidence and higher self-esteem than many of the young ladies observed for the current research, who tended to want to be recording or movie stars.

Tracey was a fifteen-year-old ninth grader when we last observed her. She was still an average student, with four C grades, a B+ in physical education, a D+, and one F grade. Four years ago when we first visited her home, Tracey was washing the dishes. She told the observer that she was involved in various fashion shows and talent shows, and had a choir rehearsal that evening. Tracey is a busy young lady, but she did no homework, and her mother did not ask about school. Her home was quiet and orderly, however. During another visit, Tracey was cleaning the house, but never did any homework. We did not observe either of her parents helping her with any schoolwork or asking about the work, despite what Ms. Love told us in the interview.

Tracey appeared to be a confident, internally controlled young lady and her mother stressed discipline and responsibility. She was involved in extracurricular activities, but we saw little stress upon schoolwork or high educational aspirations. In the more recent interview, Tracey indicated that she expected to receive a master's degree in chemistry or a related science field, which suggests high educational goals. However, her grade in biology was a C. Her goals do not appear consistent with her performance at this point. She indicated that her parents support her in terms of education, but cannot help her much since they were taught in a different educational system. It is really not the help with schoolwork by the parents that is so important but the gesture, which sends a message to the child of the importance of the work and of the child. Tracey, when asked whom she would be if she could be anyone else, still would be herself.

Ms. Love told us this time that she still encourages Tracey to do well in school by talking to her and asking questions, by going to conferences, and by encouraging programs that help students focus upon their futures. She likes the curriculum of the school, but feels that the school caters to members of certain groups. She also feels that Tracey can do well if she wants to do well, but that she likes to watch the television too much. So, she thinks that Tracey can control her own educational life, but she does not seem to be inclined to intervene with her to limit the watching of television, which has an impact upon schoolwork. This time, she did not mention peer pressure at all, but noted that Tracey talks on the telephone "too much." It is part of her responsibility to limit this if she believes that it is an impediment, which she does.

Ms. Love still stresses values, morals, respect, and God in raising Tracey. This time, we did observe Tracey doing some homework, but she talked with the observer about watching the television and playing basketball when the academic year ended, and interrupted her homework several times to check on dinner during one visit. In fact, she alternately ate the dinner and did her homework, not the best situation for the work. The house was still quiet, though neither parent asked Tracey about her work or her day.

Tracey's parents do not appear to pay much direct attention to her schoolwork, but they do emphasize discipline and responsibility. Tracey does her schoolwork, though perhaps not in the best environment. Her home environment appears to have changed little over the four years, and neither have her grades. Her family is loving and caring, though not as helpful or supportive as they might be. Little has changed over the years.

ANGOLIQUE WEAVER

When we first met Angolique, she was a thirteen-year-old eighth grader at the local middle school. Her grades were as follows: two Bs, one B-, two Cs, and one D. She also received an A in chorus, and I classified her as an average student, though I can understand why some might consider her somewhat above average. Compared to the other students observed at that time, however, she was average. When we met her for the second time, she was a sixteen-year-old junior at the high school that serves Evanston. Her grades were an A in an algebra support class, a C in algebra, a B+, a B-, a C+, a C, and a D. So, compared to her peers, she it still an average to slightly above-average student.

Four years ago, her mother, Ms. Weaver, said that Angolique's education was very important because she did not want her to go to work at McDonald's or to become a "statistic." She wanted her to go somewhere in life. She encouraged her to do well in school by helping her study, and by letting her know that extra work meant learning extra. She told us that she tries to instill discipline, respect, and self-esteem into Angolique, suggesting that she is aware of the importance of discipline and self-esteem in the educational process. A number of the parents of poor black and poor Latino students are not aware of the importance of these variables and cannot therefore work on them without some intervention.

Ms. Weaver made a very interesting point when asked whether she had anything else to say to us. She told us that she would be interested to learn the outcome of that first study so that she might learn the effects of household differences on school performance and on life. Ms. Weaver was a very perceptive mother, and her daughter was a good student.

Angolique was involved in the school chorus and aware that she was doing well in school. She pointed out that her education was very important because it would help her to get through life. Her parents, according to her, taught her that education was very important, suggesting that her parents are involved to some degree in the preparation process. She devoted about two and a half hours a night to her homework, which seems to be more than the average eighth grader at that time, and wanted to receive a master's degree. When asked what was most impor-tant in her life, she said that it was education and her family. Clark (1983) also found that family was very important in the lives of those do-ing well in school. This importance allows the family to influence the values, beliefs, and behavior of the student, and allows them to prepare the student for school if the parents know what to do and how to do it.

According to Angolique, her parents helped her "every day" with her schoolwork, and if she could change one thing about her family life, it would have been that her parents would have not been so hard on her. Ms. Weaver was observed helping Angolique with her math homework the first time that we visited their home, and Mr. Weaver reminded her to do her homework when she stopped to play with her younger sisters. The house was quiet when we next visited, with the television off, and Ms. Weaver sit-ting at a table working with a four-year-old on the alphabet. So she was al-ready teaching the young child the importance of education. The young-ster was learning to read, and Angolique was helping to teach her.

Ms. Weaver asked Angolique about her homework and asked to see her social studies work, only to be told by Angolique that she had left the homework and her books in her school locker. Ms. Weaver "calmly" told her not to leave her books at school. When the four-year-old began to play, she was scolded by her mother for playing rather than working on the words that she was being taught. During the next visit, Angolique, her sister, and the observer walked to a local grocery store, but when they returned, Ms. Weaver asked the younger sister about her home-work, and Angolique began her homework, which she did without in-terruption for about an hour before the observer left.

When Mr. Weaver arrived home during the next visit, Angolique and her cousin and siblings were listening to music, and he told them to turn the music off right away. Angolique then began her homework, with her mother "peeking over [her] shoulder while she was doing her home-work." She also helped her nephew with his homework by "giving him context clues, and by helping him with word association." Clearly, Ms. Weaver took the role of teacher at home seriously, and performed the job well. The house was quiet, the children were responsible and disci-plined, both parents consistently showed concern about schoolwork, and Ms. Weaver was prepared to help with the work.

During the next visit, Angolique discussed school with the observer, and at one point Angolique looked at the observer's notebooks, asking her questions about certain assignments that she had. The observer noted, "There wasn't much noise, it was calm and everyone was content in their own worlds." Apparently, Angolique had completed her homework before the observer arrived at 6:15 p.m. When the observer arrived for the next visit at 5:00 p.m., Angolique was working on her homework. Mr. Weaver arrived a few minutes later with the four-year-old, and he and Angolique began a conversation about what happened to her at school and at Family Focus that day. She had apparently been told while at Family Focus that she was good with younger children, but according to the observer, "he did not really give the proud response that maybe her mother would have [given]." This suggests that Ms. Weaver did in reality pay attention to the self-esteem of Angolique, as she indicated that she did in answering the questionnaire.

Angolique soon returned to her homework, but began a discussion with the observer about being able to complete the homework at school rather than bringing it home. Ms. Weaver went over her homework and pointed out the errors, telling her that Angolique would correct them when she returned from the grocery store. In summarizing her observations, the observer wrote, "My family maintained a certain amount of normalcy. . . . Important things like cooking and eating dinner together, talking as opposed to yelling, and playfulness between the parents and children were some of the things that I witnessed on almost every visit." The home environment was calm, the parents played a role in the education of the student, postsecondary education was expected, there were clear-cut rules in the home, and a great deal of sibling interaction, all characteristics of the homes of high-achieving poor blacks, according to Clark (1983). Angolique's achievement was on the border between high achieving and average.

The home environment was conducive to high achievement and the parents did most of the things needed by parents to properly prepare their student for school. As a result, their daughter, Angolique, did quite well in school.

When we visited her the second time, Angolique again told us that her family and school were the most important things in her life, and that money possibly could get in the way of her education. This suggests that she was thinking beyond high school; remember that high educational aspirations are a characteristic of higher achievers. She said that she devotes two hours a day to her schoolwork, and that she does volunteer work. She still expects to receive a master's degree, her father helps her with her math homework while her mother helps her with her history, English, and Spanish work, and they make certain that her homework gets done.

She would like for her family to have more money and a bigger house, and would be herself if she could be any one person in the world. She likes to volunteer and to bowl, and studies sign language because she is interested. She is still a confident, inquisitive young lady with high educational goals, and a fair amount of discipline. When the observer arrived for the first visit during the second set of observations, Angolique was at her computer working on a paper, and both of her two sisters were doing their homework as well. Ms. Weaver admonished Angolique for her failure to take the trash out, and suggested to the other sisters that they help her with dinner preparation. The siblings helped each other with their homework while Ms. Weaver prepared the dinner in the kitchen.

A little later Mr. Weaver arrived with the youngest addition to the family, a young boy, and asked the boy to read to him out loud. Nothing much appears to have changed in the intervening years. The youngest child is being taught to read, and the parents are actively involved in the process. Angolique finished her math homework and at her mother's orders began her Spanish homework, with her mother quizzing her on the pronunciation of several words. A younger sister was playing on the computer at this time, but her mother told her that what she had typed were not words. She told her to go into another room to get a book and retype the words. The parents remain very much involved in the teaching process. Indeed, Mr. Weaver asked one daughter to read aloud to him, and when she made a mistake to look up the word in the dictionary.

Mr. Weaver told the observer that the television could not be turned on while the children did their homework, which seemed to be almost all of the time. Indeed, according to Mr. Weaver, they are sometimes awake past midnight working on homework. During another visit, the radio was on while the sisters talked and played, but neither parent was at home initially. The radio remained on after the parents arrived and while Angolique worked on a paper for class. Soon, Mr. and Ms. Weaver left to attend an award ceremony at the school of the young boy. They appear to be still very much concerned about the education of their children, though perhaps a bit more accepting now than four years ago. The home environment is not quite as quiet or orderly, but education still seems to be the centerpiece in this household. Little has changed in the Weaver household over the years, and Angolique is still a good student.

PIERRE BAROQUE

Four years ago, Pierre was a twelve-year-old sixth grader at a middle school located outside of the neighborhood in which all of the students observed lived. His grades were classified as average, though they were borderline and could have been considered below average. He received three C- grades, and three grades of D, along with a B in a technology course. He lived with his mother, a single mother, and one other child. Ms. Baroque, like all of the parents in all of my studies, believed that Pierre's education was very important because it would allow him to succeed in life. She said then that she encouraged him to do well by studying with him and by letting him know that making mistakes was acceptable as long as he learned from the mistakes.

She indicated that Pierre's inability to set goals and lack of self-control got in the way of his getting a good education, demonstrating that she placed the responsibility upon Pierre rather than on external factors. In raising Pierre, she said that she stressed discipline and the enforcement of a set of rules. Pierre told us that he most liked his after-school activities about school, that he devotes one to three hours a day on his homework, and that his family was the most important thing in his life. His mother helped with his schoolwork "a lot," according to him, and this was enough help for him. Pierre told us that he wanted to attend graduate school and that he expected to do so. He had rather high educational aspirations, especially given his mediocre grades.

When the observer arrived at the Baroque home for the third visit (the first observation took place at Family Focus, and Pierre was not at home during the second visit), Pierre was doing his homework at the kitchen table while Ms. Baroque prepared a bath for his younger brother. Ms. Baroque asked Pierre the due date of his homework, and then asked to see his math textbook, complaining that he needed to become better organized. Later he asked his mother a question about his work, and when he had difficulty with another problem his mother told him that she did not know the answer and that he should look in his book. Pierre got up to find an encyclopedia and used the telephone. When his mother realized that he was on the telephone rather than doing his homework, "she freaks out." She yelled at him three times to get off the telephone.

Ms. Baroque seemed to require discipline of Pierre, though yelling at him may not have been the best approach. On the other hand, when Ms. Baroque asked Pierre about his science homework several times, he nevertheless failed to do the work. She was upset with his failure to organize his school papers in his backpack and let him know this, organizing the papers for him. Later, she asked him about the school student council and why he was not selected to participate on the council. Ms. Baroque was involved in Pierre's schoolwork, and very interested in and concerned about his school activity. During another visit, Pierre again asked his mother for her help with his homework, and again, she had difficulty with the issue herself, but nevertheless figured out the answer and helped him. The key to the parent-as-teacher role at home is that the parent consistently help the student, which lets the student know the value of the work and the value that a parent has of the student. The actual help is not as important as the message that it sends to the student.

Throughout our visits, the Baroque home was reasonably quiet and orderly, despite the fact that Pierre's younger brother was present and occasionally made the type of fuss made by youngsters. Ms. Baroque consistently limited the amount of noise and playing she would tolerate from him, though. Pierre was participating with the school newspaper at that time, as well as the school band. In fact, he told the observer that he was the best in the band with his instrument, suggesting high self-esteem. On one occasion he made a cake at home, with some direction from his mother. According to the observer, "[Ms. Baroque] is always commanding," at various times telling Pierre to "pick up this stuff, get off the bed." "[Pierre], you have stuff to do" "Change the fish water."

"Put all the papers in their place." This discipline is much needed in poor communities and for poor nonwhite students.

Pierre was a confident young man whose mother was very much involved almost nightly with his schoolwork. She demanded discipline and responsibility from him while working full time and caring for a younger child as well as Pierre. He was involved in a variety of extracurricular activities, including the school paper, the band, and basketball, all of which promote discipline, responsibility, and higher self-esteem. It was, however, not clear that Pierre attached the same level of importance to his schoolwork that his mother seemed to do. He may have not received the message sent by his mother, but his household seemed to be a middle-class, though poor, household, and Pierre was an average, though borderline, student.

When we next saw Pierre, he was a fifteen-year-old freshman at the local high school, and still an average student. He had one B+ grade, one C+, one C, and two D+ grades, so I would say that he is still an average student. This time, Ms. Baroque told us that Pierre's education was "real important" because she does not want him to struggle, and she wants him to get a good job. Like the parents of most of the average and below-average students, she seemed to link education more to the job market than to self-development or knowledge. She said that she encourages him to do well in school by telling him how important school is, by admonishing him to not procrastinate, to keep his grades up, and by telling him how smart he is. This last statement indicates her concern with Pierre's self-esteem, which is, of course, good. However, if the grades that Pierre received for his last grading period are considered good, then Ms. Baroque does not have very high expectations of him.

Ms. Baroque pointed out that only Pierre can hold himself back in terms of receiving a good education, that his outspokenness gets him in trouble, and that he needs to learn to keep his opinion to himself. This tells me that she wants Pierre to be in control of his life, an indication of her concern with internal control, and also of her concern with his discipline, both of which are keys to high academic achievement. In fact, she mentioned that self-esteem was important in raising Pierre. She also mentioned that being a single parent was difficult. She did not need to mention that being a black, poor single parent is extremely difficult.

Still, at least in the past, she did a number of the things required of families if their children are to perform well in school.

Pierre is involved in the theater at school, and now believes that he is doing fair in school, which is an accurate understanding of his performance. Education is still important to him, only now this is the case because "it is better to learn now rather than later." He now does most of his homework at school because he has two study halls at school, and he saves the "easy" homework for home. He wants to attend college and to become an actor. He says that he is the only real obstacle in the way of his achieving his educational expectations, because he has a problem with authority, that he is very outspoken about defending his views. This is, of course, the concern of his mother as well, but given that they are both aware of the problem it would seem that they would do something about it, and that this is the responsibility of Ms. Baroque to a considerable extent.

Pierre told us that it is most important that he achieve his goals and that he feels good about himself, again suggesting his level of confidence and self-esteem. He told us this time that he receives no help with his schoolwork from his mother, while four years ago he indicated that he received a lot of help from her. Of course, if he actually does most of his work at school she cannot help him, but she could monitor the work and ask about the work.

When the observer arrived for the first visit during the second set of observations, Pierre was watching the television, and when Ms. Baroque arrived from the store she explained to the observer that they could not meet on two days of the week because the family attended church on both of those days, which tells us that religion is still important to the family. When the younger boy, now nine years of age, asked to join other boys in attending a talent show at a local school and failed to say goodbye to the observer, Ms. Baroque told him that he must learn manners and required him to say goodbye to the observer. She still establishes clear role boundaries with her children, though during the visit Pierre did no homework and Ms. Baroque did not ask about school or schoolwork. This was very different from that which we observed several years ago.

When the observer arrived for the next visit, Pierre was vacuuming the rug. When he completed this housework, he laid down on the floor in front of the television to work on a school project. Ms. Baroque reminded him that he still had chores to complete and that it was not acceptable to do homework with the television on. So, she still pays attention to Pierre's schoolwork and still tries to maintain a quiet, structured home environment, though Pierre told her that the project really was not homework, which should allow him to complete the work while watching the television.

Pierre then asked his mother whether he could use bleach on his shoes in the washer, and Ms. Baroque replied that this was acceptable as long as he also put his blanket in with the shoes. He put the wrong blanket in the washer and he and his mother had some disagreement about how to deal with this situation. When he asked to put a different pair of shoes in the washer and his mother refused to allow this, he protested, telling her that he had used his own money to purchase the shoes and could do with them what he liked, clearly challenging her authority, something rarely seen in the homes of high achievers. Ms. Baroque told him that he could not wash the shoes using "my water, my bleach," reestablishing her authority.

Later, Pierre began a discussion with the observer about college in which he assumed that he would attend college. In fact, he talked about "when" he attended college, and not "if" he attended, as though it were a foregone conclusion, suggesting high educational expectations. He later returned to his school project.

When the observer next arrived, Ms. Baroque was cooking dinner while the younger son worked on his homework at the kitchen table. Though he constantly asked to go outdoors to play, Ms. Baroque was adamant that he complete the homework first, a good lesson in delayed gratification. When he asked her for help, she attempted to help without answering the questions for him, another characteristic of the homes of high achievers. She wanted him to have to think through the questions. When he expressed dissatisfaction with her approach, she told him that he was smart enough to do the work on his own, and to "sit his butt down and finish those questions." When he turned to the observer for the answers, she told him immediately that this was not acceptable.

When the youngster again asked to go outside, indicating that the work was done, Ms. Baroque decided to check it for herself. When satisfied that he had in fact done the work, she complimented him, but did not allow him to go outside. Pierre arrived soon after and Ms. Baroque asked right away how his school day had gone. When he indicated that he had been selected to be involved in an extracurricular activity, she congratulated him as well. She asked about his homework, even asked to see his book bag, something she did several years ago as well, and again complained about his lack of organization. Ms. Baroque is a consistent parent who does most of the things needed to properly prepare students for the school experience, and she is doing those things with both boys.

Pierre then went into his mother's bedroom to use the telephone to call his father, who lives in another state. Ms. Baroque had told Pierre that he could make the call if he completed all of his household chores over the weekend, a very good way to teach responsibility, and the ability to delay gratification.

The Baroque children are involved in the type of positive activities with their mother that Furstenberg et al. (1999) found to be associated with positive adolescent development. Ms. Baroque has established the type of clear role boundaries that Clark (1983) found to be associated with high achievers. Furthermore, she provides nurturance and support; the quiet, structured, orderly home environment; the words to support higher self-esteem on the part of her children; the help with schoolwork, which is critical; and the expectation that the boys will play a role in their own education. Pierre is involved in doing household chores and in extracurricular activities. Most of the characteristics of the students in high-achieving households are in place in this home and have been over time—yet Pierre is not a high achiever, and has not been one. His grades have been consistently average. It may be that his tendency to be outspoken and to challenge authority keeps his grades low. If this is the case, it seems that it is Ms. Baroque's responsibility to teach him to curb this tendency, and as he has grown older, his as well.

On the other hand, I am not certain that if this is the case, it should be. That is, teachers should not really hold this against him, if they in fact do so. Outspoken young black males can be intimidating to many in our society, however, and many pay a heavy price for this. They should not have to do so, but they must be aware of their image and the reaction to this on the part of others.

The Baroque household is an example of a solidly middle-class poor black home in which the parent, almost always the mother, works full time, and spends a great deal of time and energy playing the role not only of mother but also of teacher at home. Her interaction with her children is positive and supportive, Pierre expects to receive a postsecondary education, and is a confident, self-assured young student with high education expectations. Given his current grades, those expectations seem unrealistic, but given the values, attitudes, and behavior of his mother, I would not rule them out.

CAMILLE DUNN

Camille Dunn was a fifteen-year-old ninth grader at the high school when we observed her family several years ago, and a low-achieving student, with two C grades, two D+ grades, and a D grade. She received an F in physical education as well. Her mother, Ms. Dunn, thought that Camille's education was very important because she wanted to see her go to college and "make something of herself." She told us that she tried to encourage Camille to do well by helping her with her homework and by teaching her to assert herself. She said that she did not visit Camille's school often, but that when she did visit she felt happy because Camille was having fun, "that's what's important." It occurs to me that having fun, while nice, is not a reason for the parent of a high school student to feel happy about visiting the school. There are many more important things about high school than having fun.

Ms. Dunn noted that the only things that she believed stood in Camille's way in terms of her receiving a good education were her interest in boys and the lack of money. In response to the question about what she most liked about school, by the way, Camille listed boys. They both seem aware that her interest in boys is a high priority for Camille. In discussing how she raised Camille, Ms. Dunn told us that it was difficult to discipline teenagers, and that she stresses respect.

Camille believed then that she was doing well in school, despite her grades, and that education was very important to her as well, "because I need to have an education." This was a very general answer for a fifteen-year-old, perhaps suggesting a lack of focus on her part. Camille said that she devoted one and a half to two hours a day to her homework, that she wanted to attend graduate school, and that she expects to do so. She had high education aspirations, especially considering her grades. In fact, the goal seemed unrealistic at that time. She indicated that her family and school were the most important things in her life, and that her parents helped her "a lot" with her schoolwork.

During our visits, however, we never observed her doing any schoolwork, nor did Ms. Dunn ask about school or show interest in Camille's day or activities. Ms. Dunn drank beer during two of our visits, and as I wrote earlier (Sampson 2002) "Camille appears to be raising herself." She and her sister prepared dinner for themselves, and were comfortable with people selling and using drugs near their apartment. When at Family Focus, there was no talk of school or homework, only talk of boys and sex. There were, in fact, none of the characteristics of the homes of higher achievers observed; indeed, we saw relatively little home life at all, and there was little to indicate that Camille actually attended school. Her mother was not typically in the home when Camille was there, so she could offer her very little help, and Camille was clearly not interested in school or in her education.

When we visited Camille for the second set of observations, she was an eighteen-year-old who said that she was in the eleventh or twelfth grade at the high school. It appears that she should have been in the twelfth grade, but did not have the credits to be placed there. Her grades were two Cs, a C-, and three F grades, still a low-achieving student. Ms. Dunn still indicates that Camille's education is very important, "because without school you won't get far." She encourages Camille to do well by telling her to stay in school as long as she can, and believes that Camille is doing "very well in school." Obviously, she is not in touch with Camille's school life. She went on to tell us that Camille's "grades are wonderful." Her daughter is failing almost half of her courses, and she believes that this is "wonderful." Either she does not know anything about how Camille is doing or she thinks that F grades are acceptable, even "wonderful." If it is the former, she is not doing her job as the teacher of Camille at home. If the latter, she has very low expectations of her daughter, and her daughter seems to live down to those expectations.

Camille believes that she is doing very well in school, so she too is either out of touch or has very low expectations. She said that she believes that some teachers are too hard on her, and that education is still very important to her. She does not have much homework, and still expects to attend college and to receive a master's degree. At this point, even high school graduation does not seem to be assured.

Most of the time that the observer spent at Camille's home during the first visit, she and her mother were at a table listening to music. Camille did tell the observer of her interest in possibly attending a local trade school or beauty school, raising more questions about her stated interest in a master's degree and about her knowledge of the academic world. While in the home this first time, the observer noted that a number of friends of Camille and her teenaged sister arrived, and talked with the girls. Most of the discussion involved hairstyles and boys, never school or homework or their future.

During the next visit, the observer walked with Camille and her sisters to a hair store where they bought hair to be used for hair weaves. Back at home, the television remained on during the entire visit. He wrote, "The next hour or two of my visit were spent with hair everywhere," in reference to the weaving that went on in the house. Ms. Dunn "asked around" for beer money, indicating that she still drinks beer. There was no mention of school during the five-hour visit.

When the observer arrived for the next visit, Camille and her sisters were at McDonald's picking up their dinner, but they returned soon, only to begin the hair-weaving process again. Ms. Dunn came downstairs and again asked her daughters for money, this time to buy something else. The observer noted that during his visits he had not observed any of the three girls doing any schoolwork, nor did any adult mention schoolwork, nor was there any kind of routine that centered on schoolwork or reading. A number of friends and relatives come and go all day and evening; on this evening, "The girls mostly sat and worked on each other's weaves and talked about different boys. Normally who was sleeping with who." These are teenaged girls talking in front of their mother and aunt, though Ms. Dunn pops in and out of the house often.

The Dunn household appears to be the opposite of the homes of the academic high achievers. There is no involvement in extracurricular activates, indeed, little evidence of involvement in school by any of the students; no involvement with the children by either parent; no supervision of their activities; no specific role boundaries; no orderly environment;

little discipline; no educational expectations; no homework; and, of course, no help with the nonexistent homework. This is the case for all three girls in the home. There is no evidence of the ability to delay gratification on the part of the student or her mother, and none of the type of parent–student interactions that influence achievement mentioned by Murphy (2003). There is little wonder that Camille is doing so poorly.

SUMMARY

I began this research with essentially three goals: to compare and contrast the role of family patterns, values, and beliefs on the achievement of poor black and poor Latino students; expand the research on the relationship of the family dynamic to the academic achievement of poor blacks and poor Latinos; and, finally, reexamine family patterns and achievement some four years after the initial examination to determine whether achievement levels and family patterns have changed over time.

It appears that the family dynamic and its relationship to the academic achievement of students is much the same for poor blacks and poor Latinos, though it is clear that language plays a major role in affecting the achievement of some Latino students due in large part to the limitations that it places on the involvement with and understanding of the schoolwork and school activities of the students. It is also possible that there are some cultural differences between non-Latinos and Latinos with regard to child-rearing patterns and gender.

Given that the nature of the research on the role of the family in the education of students imposes limits on the number of students and families studied, and the fact that the research is relatively new, more research is needed in order to increase our confidence in the findings. While the research on the topic has yielded very similar results, the number of families and students involved has been quite small, causing some to question the validity of the findings. The numbers are beginning to allow more confidence in the findings, but I reasoned that we needed even more research. For the current work, I observed seventeen new families, and reobserved five families that had been observed several years earlier. I am quite confident that we know what parents need to do in the home in order to positively impact the academic achievement of poor black and poor Latino students.

Finally, as to the question of whether the academic achievement level of the students observed four years ago has changed, the answer is, apparently, no. Further, the family behavior and the parenting behavior have not changed much either. The parents seem to be doing that which they did four years ago when their children were younger, and the grades of their children are about the same. The family dynamic seems to remain steady, and as a result, the grades seem to do the same.

This research is very difficult to do. Finding poor families that are willing to allow strangers into their homes for hours at a time for weeks is not easy. Many poor families have things that they would rather the world not know. They often have very small and cramped living environments. They sometimes have little food or furniture. Adults often have no jobs. There is often a single parent working full time, especially in the homes of poor blacks, and that parent must find the time and energy to be a teacher at home. The observers must be respectful, patient, and nonjudgmental. Much is asked of the families, and much is required of the observers. Nevertheless, I have found many poor Latino and poor black families willing to allow this intrusion. Now we need to begin to find those willing to allow us to show them what is needed to better prepare their children for school. We know what it takes.

BIBLIOGRAPHY

WORKS CITED

Baron, A., and M. Vasquez. 1990. *Parents and schools: Success through partnership. A presentation guide for school administration and service.* ERIC Document ED 358 185.

Bempechat, A. W. 1998. *Against the odds: How "at risk" children exceed expectations.* San Francisco: Jossey-Bass.

Boykin, A. W. 1986. The triple quandry and the schooling of Afro-American children. In *The school achievement of minority children,* edited by U. Neisser, 57–92. Hillsdale, N.J.: Lawrence Erlbaum.

Clark, R. M. 1983. *Family life and school acievement: Why poor black children succeed or fail.* Chicago: University of Chicago Press.

Coleman, J. S., et al. 1966. *Equality of educational opportunity.* Washington, D.C.: U.S. Office of Education.

Comer, J. P. 1993. Inner-city education: A theoretical and intervention model. In *Sociology and the public agenda,* edited by W. J. Wilson. Newbury Park, Calif: Sage.

Darder, A., R. D. Torres, and H. Gutierrez. 1992. *Latinos and education: A critical Reader.* New York: Routledge.

Delgado-Gaitan, C. 1992. School matters in the Mexican-American home: Socializing children to education. *American Educational Research Journal* 29 (3): 495–513.

Edmonds, R. 1979. Effective schools for the urban poor. *Educational Leadership* 37:15–23.

Ford, D. 1993. Black students' achievement orientation as a function of percieved family achievement orientation and demographic variables. *Journal of Negro Education* 62 (1).

Fordham, S., and J. U. Ogbu. 1986. Black students' school success: Coping with the burden of "acting white." *Urban Review* 18 (3): 1–31.

Furstenberg, F. F. Jr., et.al. 1999. *Managing to make it: Urban families and adolescent success*. Chicago: University of Chicago Press.

Goodenow, C., and K. E. Grady. 1994. The relationship of school belonging and friends' values to academic motivation among urban adolescent students. *Journal of Experimental Education* 62:60–71.

Graff, G. 2003. Interview with *Chicago Tribune*, June 20.

Gutman, L., and V. McLoyd. 2000. Parents' management of their childrens' education within the home, at school, and in the community: An examination of African-Americans families living in poverty. *Urban Review* 32 (1).

Grossman, H. 1995. *Educating Hispanic students: Implications for instruction, classroom management, counseling, and assement*. Springfield, Ill.: Charles C. Thomas.

Harrington, C. C., and S. K. Boardman. 1997. *Paths to success: Beating the odds in American society*. Cambridge: Harvard University Press.

Howell, W. G., and P. E. Peterson. 2002. *The education gap: Vouchers and urban schools*. Washington, D.C.: Brookings Institution Press.

Howard, J. J., and R. Hammond. 1985. Rumors of inferiority. *New Republic* 193:17–21.

Ianni, F. A. J. 1987. Revisiting school-community responsibilities in the administration of education. In *Educating black children: America's challenge,* edited by D. S. Strickland and E. J. Cooper, 2–18. Washington, D.C.: Howard University Press.

Irvine, J. J. 1991. *Black students and school failure*. Westport, Conn.: Praeger.

Jackson, P. 2004. A call to bridge the gap: Race and the discrepancy in academic achievement. In *Afrique Newsmagazine* (May).

Jencks, C., et al. 1972. *Inequality: A reassement of the effect of family and schooling in America*. New York: Basic Books.

Kozol, J. 1991. *Savage inequalities: Children in America's schools*. New York: Crown.

Lareau, A. 1989. *Home advantage: Social class and parental intervention in elementary education*. New York: Falmer Press.

———. 2000. *Home advantage: Social class and parental intervention in elementary education*. Lanham, Md.: Rowman and Littlefield.

Lightfoot, S. 1978. *Worlds apart: Relationships between families and schools.* New York: Basic Books.

Moynihan, D. P. 1965. *The Negro family: The case for national action.* Washington, D.C.: Office of Policy Planning and Research, U.S. Department of Labor.

Murphy, J. C. 2003. Case studies in African-American school success and parenting behaviors. *Young Children* (November).

National Commission on Excellence in Education. 1983. *A nation at risk: The imperative for education reform.* Washington, D.C.: U.S. Department of Education.

Ogbu, J. 1978. *Minority education and caste: The American system in cross-cultural perspective.* New York: Academic Press.

———. 2003. *Black American students in an affluent suburb: A study of academic disengagement.* Mahwah, N.J.: Erlbaum.

Sampson, W. A. 2002. *Black student achievement: How much do family and school really matter?* Lanham, Md.: Scarecrow Press.

———. 2003. *Poor Latino families and school preparation: Are they doing the right things?* Lanham, Md.: Scarecrow Press.

Sanchez, G. 1997. History, culture, and education. In *Latinos and education,* edited by A. Darder, R. D. Torres, and H. Guiterrez. New York: Routledge.

Slavin, R., N. Karweit, and N. Madden. 1989. *Effective programs for students at risk.* Needham Heights, Mass.: Allyn and Bacon.

Tapia, J. 2000. Schooling and learning in U.S.-Mexican families: A case study of households. *Urban Review* 32 (1).

Trueba, H. 1988. Culturally based explanations of minority student's academic achievement. *Anthropology and Education Quarterly* 19:270–85.

Valdes, S. 1998. The effect of Mexican immigrant parents on their children's academic achievement in American schools. Master's thesis, Depaul University, Chicago, Ill.

Valencia, R., ed. 1991. *Chicano school failure and success: Research and policy agendas for the 1990s.* New York: Falmer Press.

Weis, L. 1985. *Between two worlds: Black students in an urban community college.* Boston, Mass.: Routledge and Kegan Paul.

Wrigly, J. 2000. Foreword. *Home advantage: Social class and parental intervention in elementary education.* Lanham, Md.: Rowman and Littlefield.

Wilson, W. J. *The truly disadvantaged: The inner city, the underclass, and public policy.* Chicago: University of Chicago Press.

Whittington, D. 1996. Analysis of underachievement. Unpublished document, Shaker Heights School District, Shaker Heights, Ohio.

ADDITIONAL SOURCES

Borstein, M., ed. 1995. *Children and parenting.* Vol. 1 of *Handbook of parenting.* Mahwah, N.J.: Erlbaum.

Brooks-Gunn, J. 1995. Strategies for altering the outcomes of poor children and their families. In *Escape from poverty: What makes a difference for children?* edited by P. L. C. Landsdale and J. B. Gunn. Cambridge: Cambridge University Press.

Coleman, J. S. 1981. *The adolescent society.* Westport, Conn.: Greenwood Press.

Comer, J. P. 1988. Educating poor minority children. *Scientific American* 256 (11): 42–48.

Christenson, S., and S. Sheridan. 2001. *Schools and families: Creating essential connections for learning.* New York: Guilford Press.

Epstein, J. 1987. Parental involvement: What research says to administrators. *Education and Urban Society* 19:119–36.

Ianni, F. A. J. 1987. Revisiting school-community responsibilites in the admistration of education. In *Educating black children: America's challenge,* edited by D. S. Strickland and E. J. Cooper, 2–18. Washington, D.C.: Howard University Press.

Jencks, C., and S. Mayer. 1990. The social consequences of growing up in a poor neighborhood. In *Inner-city poverty in the United States,* edited by L. E. Lyman and M. G. H. McGeary. Washington, D.C.: National Academy Press.

Kotlowitz, A. 1991. *There are no children here.* New York: Doubleday.

Lane, R. 1995. The perils of school vouchers. In *Rethinking schools: An agenda for change,* edited by D. Levine et al. New York: New Press.

Lewis, O. 1959. *Five families: Mexican case studies in the culture of poverty.* New York: Basic Books.

Mackler, B. 1971. Blacks who are academically successful. *Urban Education* 5:210–37.

Macleod, J. 1987. *Ain't no making it: Aspirations and attainment in a low-income neighborhood.* Boulder, Colo.: Westview Press.

McAdoo, H. P., and J. L. McAdoo. 1985. *Black children: Social, educational, and parental enviorments.* Beverly Hills, Calif.: Sage.

Neisser, U. 1986. *The school achievement of minority children.* Hillsdale, N.J.: Erlbaum.

Ogbu, J. 1988. Class stratification, racial stratification, and schooling. In *Class, race, and gender in American education,* edited by L. Weis, 163–82. Albany: State University of New York Press.

Scott-Jones, D. 1987. Mother as teacher in the families of high and low achieving first graders. *Journal of Negro* Education 56 (1): 21–34.

Walberg, H. 1984. Families as partners in educational productivity. *Phi Delta Kappan* 65: 397–400.

Weis, L. 1992. *Schooling and the silenced "others": Race and class in schools.* Albany: State University of New York, GSE Publications.

INDEX

ABOUT THE AUTHOR

Dr. William Sampson grew up in poor, but middle-class neighborhoods in Milwaukee, Wisconsin. As was the case for many poor black students growing up during that time, he was pointed toward and supported in his academic success by many in his neighborhood.

He is currently associate professor of public policy and sociology at DePaul University and has a B.A. in sociology and psychology from Howard University; an M.A. in urban affairs from the University of Wisconsin at Milwaukee; and a PhD. in social relations from The Johns Hopkins University. Dr. Sampson has previously written *Black Student Achievement: How Much Do Family and School Really Matter?* and *Poor Latino Families and School Preparation: Are They Doing the Right Things?*